YOU MUST GO BACK

Whende Thomas

My story of dying, meeting Jesus
in heaven, and being sent back…

All rights reserved. This book is protected by the copyright laws of the United States of America. This book may not be copied or reprinted for commercial gain or profit. The use of short quotations or occasional page copying for personal or group study is permitted and encouraged. Permission will be granted upon request.

Scriptures identified as (NIV) are taken from the Holy Bible, New International Version®, Copyright © 1973, 1978, 1984 International Bible Society. Used by permission of Zondervan. All rights reserved.

Scriptures identified as (NLT) are taken from the Holy Bible, New Living Translation, Copyright © 1996, 2004. Used by permission of Tyndale House Publishers, Wheaton, Illinois 60189. All rights reserved.

Copyright © 2021 Whende Thomas

All rights reserved.

ISBN: 979-8-7354-0581-8

For Worldwide Distribution, Printed in the U.S.A.

DEDICATION

This book is dedicated to the One who supported without ceasing, who paid without hesitating, loved without boundaries, and suffered without blame. He pursued me even when I gave up on Him. He chose torture and death to redeem me. I cannot fathom any of those choices, but the hardest to conceive is that He chose to leave heaven and His Father's holy presence to do all this. Thank you, Father, Son, and Holy Spirit for finding this prodigal daughter worthy of your relentless love and forgiveness.

ACKNOWLEDGMENTS

I must first acknowledge my handsome prince, Anthony Thomas, who lived this story with me. Our journey was not easy; after heaven I felt I spoke a different language that only heaven could understand, but you never stopped trying to comprehend my journey. You loved me despite my resentment for being sent back.

To my precious children, I pray this will help you understand why I was so odd for many of your young years. Hopefully, you will understand that I wrote this largely for you and my future generations. I want nothing more than to show you heaven, so my life and desperation for everyone to love Jesus will finally make sense. Macy Lou and Louna, and any future generations who are not yet conceived, never forget God sent me back to be certain you get to heaven.

Thank you, Timmy Chatman, for your bold obedience in sharing the gifts God has given you. Your prophesy changed my life. Thank you, Jennifer, for always pushing me to be my best. Thank you, Jean Ballinger, for your constant prayers, love and confidence in me. You've taught me so much and loved me so undeservedly.

I need to acknowledge the many people who trusted God and were obedient to His requests. Had you not obeyed, I would still be chasing my tail having a pity party. Thank you for stepping out in faith and changing my life.

I must acknowledge the other prodigals who may be reading this. Perhaps you think it's too late to turn your life around, or maybe you have messed up so big that you think God would not want to redeem you. The Bible is full of people whose lives are train wrecks, yet God chooses to use them to do incredible miracles. I am living proof God still uses the imperfect to do His perfect will.

CONTENTS

FORWARD

Does anyone know what heaven is really like? Is there a life after this life? Or is this life all we get and what we face ahead is the black void of oblivion? These questions are instinctual to humans. We have an innate desire for meaning and purpose. We want to know why and how we are here. Is there a reason we are drawing breath? Whether you 're a person of faith or an atheist, we all ponder what will happen after we die. Whatever conclusions you've made, we do have this in common, we live, and we die. It is the inevitability of death that feeds our fears of the unknown, but life without hope is a dark way to live. Simply having hope for a better future makes a big difference in any person's life.

If we choose to live our life based solely on what we can see with our eyes, we have chosen a form of blindness. There are too many unexplained phenomena, too many mysteries and things we just don't understand. Even with all of our technological advances there is still so much we don't know. Living without any measure of faith in the unseen is similar to the Ostrich sticking its head in the sand. There is enough empirical evidence from people of a wide variety of backgrounds that give creed to life after death. The proof is in testimonies from individuals who clinically died but came back to life with revelations far beyond just electrical synapses of a dying brain.

If you are a truth seeker or a researcher, the assimilation of pertinent information is essential. None of us have all the answers regarding heaven. So, don't make your conclusions before you've collected enough data. It's alright to make a hypothesis, but the real seeker of truth must be willing to shift assumptions when faced with real evidence. This is my request to you the reader. There is information in this book that could alter your preconceived opinions. Be an honest scientist and listen to

Whende's story. Hear with an open heart her experience before you make up your mind. Don't allow your history of pain or disappointment keep you from allowing your heart to feel hope of something better.

Part of my journey has been a fascination with heaven. I've studied ancient Bible texts for years seeking greater insight. I've read theological books that give creed to the reality of heaven by investigating the beliefs of many cultures and generations. I've studied multiple religions and their conclusions about the afterlife. I've read many books about life and death experiences. The idea of heaven is pervasive not only in American culture, but in most cultures. As a follower of Christ, I believe heaven is in my future. It's a belief that has grown the more I've researched.

Most people like happy stories. We want the guy or gal to find true love. We hope the conflicted person will find peace. We are moved by people who experience the joy of restored relationship. Every great story involves a crisis seeking to be resolved. We can relate because each of us know the pain of a world in conflict. *You Must Go Back* is a true story that may surprise you. It is the story of Whende Thomas who died in a river accident, went to heaven, but then came back to life. I appreciate that Whende's story doesn't end with her heaven experience, but it's really just the beginning. Her amazing experience in heaven does not lead her into a life of rainbows and roses. The majority of this book is her learning to live with this new knowledge. There were dark days of discouragement grappling with the reason she was sent back. Everything in this life became bland compared to the beauty of what she experienced with Jesus in the heavenly realm. She bares her soul before us. There's no candy coating here. Her vulnerability is refreshing and disarming. She communicates in an authentic open-hearted way that has moved me to reach for more in life. Her journey reveals a person trying to make sense of the world while having firsthand knowledge of heaven. What if you could go to heaven, come back and tell people what it's like? It may sound easy, but Whende can tell you it is not.

When I first met Whende, she was visiting a ministry training school that I lead. Her personality is big, like the uniqueness of her style, but she was also cautious, skeptical and not wanting to be fooled. Her conservative upbringing had trained her to have a particular mindset regarding people who believed in the supernatural. It didn't take long for her to start telling her story of dying and going to heaven. I think she's used to the shock value of people's reaction and some who start to question her sanity. As she interacted with our team, she was disarmed by our response to her and her story. Like I said earlier I have a fascination with heaven, so her story was not an unusual subject for us. We have a strong value in bringing the reality of heaven to earth. In fact, we see it as our assignment from Jesus to demonstrate the power of heaven through the Holy Spirit every day. Our school became part of her story. She attended our school for two years and discovered other people who really want to see heaven on earth. Whende has become a powerful champion of heaven. If you ever have the privilege to meet her, she will not hold back telling you of her love for Jesus and what He could mean in your life and tell you the beauty of what await those who believe.

As a jigsaw puzzle reveals a picture as the pieces are put in place, so God reveals his plan for our life as we submit to His process. Sometimes our life feels like a big hot mess that doesn't make any sense. Whende's life kind of looked like that too. As you read this book, let her story give you faith for your story. What feels like a disconnected pile of unrelated pieces, may be God writing another beautiful story...yours!

Don Finley
Senior Pastor, Life Church
Salem, Oregon

MEETING JESUS

It was Memorial Day 1996, and I was excited that I had finally convinced my friend to go rafting the Santiam River with myself, my sister, and her husband. Memorial Day marks the annual Santiam River Run in the beautiful Cascade mountain towns of Gates, Mill City, and Lyons, Oregon. Yearly, hundreds of people concoct their crazy floatation devices made of wood, couches, or even old recliners which are strapped to numerous inner tubes. Hundreds of fun rafting parties all launch at Packsaddle Park in Gates and float down to John Neil Park in Lyons where we pull our rafts out. Then there would be a big celebration with a live band and barbeque. It was hilariously entertaining to watch the many river floaters on their ridiculous floatation inventions every year. Many were intoxicated before even launching; several would have ropes tied to their crazy floating crafts, towing numerous coolers of beer to float behind. I had made this trip many times and looked forward to the fun all year. This year would be especially great because I had a "first timer" friend with me, although she was far less enthusiastic than I was. I had to sweet talk her to get her to participate. My friend, Nancy, had never drifted the river before, but I assured her we had all the proper safety gear, including life vests, water shoes, etc. There was nothing to fear; I considered myself a seasoned veteran on this river, and this would be a great adventure.

Nancy and I were in my raft, and my sister Katrina and brother

1

in-law Mike followed in their raft. It was a chilly, cloudy morning. We were on the river for about ten minutes when I realized we still had not seen any other floaters. In addition, the water was so high and fast, that I was having a tough time navigating our position on the river. Over to the right, a man jumping up and down on the shore caught my eye; he was dressed in a police like uniform, trying wildly to get my attention and throwing rocks towards our raft. Once I realized this was an officer, it occurred to me where we were on the river. Typically, when a rafter enters Spencer's Hole, there is an immediate awareness because a rocky wall is marked with a few ominous memorial plaques of people who have died there. After this awareness happens, many rafters pull the raft out of the water before the drop and port the rafts to re-enter the river about fifty feet beyond the small but dangerous drop. This, of course, had always been my plan. However, in 1996 the Santiam Canyon had experienced some extensive flooding causing river water to be swollen well above the rocks. My friend was laughing and asking me what this idiot cop was doing trying to get our attention, but the look of panic in my eyes was enough to convey my terrified thoughts. I immediately realized we were exactly where we were never supposed to be. Franticly, I quickly scrambled about the raft in a panic. But there was nothing I could do to get us to shore to avoid the terrifying drop, so I screamed for my friend to hold on tight. I searched for my baby sister and brother-in-law, and I was momentarily relieved they were a safe distance behind us, hung up on a rock. My relief only lasted a split second because the river was far too loud for them to hear my warning screams.

Out of my control, we crested the top of the drop which is typically a small but treacherous dip, but this day it felt more like a waterfall. It was at that moment right before we were about to plummet down that hungry, swollen drop that I realized, that my selfish adrenaline junkie needs may potentially kill my friend (a mother of two young girls) and me. Surely, we would not survive this raging plummet. Spencer's Hole is dangerous on a good day, and this was a very bad day; in fact, it had just become the worst

2

of bad days. I will never forget the look of terror and betrayal on my dear friend's face as she realized this was a big drop we were beginning to descend, and there was a very good chance she and I were not going to survive it. As the raft dove into the torrent, it felt as though we were in slow motion. So many thoughts were rushing through my head, and I immediately began praying the minute we started down, "God what have I done? Have I sentenced my friend to death? What have I done? She has small children. I have small children. God forgive me. What have I done?"

I'm a severe asthmatic, and I'm not a very strong swimmer nor can I hold my breath for more than 18 seconds, but this fact was the last thing on my mind. As my body hit the frigid water, I was forced down deep into a whirlpool, being pulled down so deep that I could no longer see light coming through the water. I felt as though I was being flushed into an upside-down toilet bowl. My body spun round and round like a brick in a washing machine as my head banged against the surface of the jagged cauldron. I was more terrified than I'd ever been in my life. Survival being my only thought, my prayers became entirely selfish. "God help me. How can I survive this? You can't take me. Who will raise my babies? My husband won't raise them to love You, so you can't take me. Don't take me. Please God. Spare me. Spare my friend. Don't let us die. God only you can save us. PLEASE SAVE US." It felt like the devil himself was pulling me to the darkest, deepest bowels of hell. I felt defenseless, out of control, and abandoned by God.

It was only a matter of seconds, before I knew I was about to die. I started praying as loud as I could in my heart, screaming in my spirit: "'Our Father who art in heaven,' God, please save me. 'How precious is your name.' Jesus save me. 'Thy kingdom come' I'm going to die, and I can't hold my breath another moment. 'Thy will be done.' Please, Father, don't take me. This can't be your will. 'On Earth as it is in heaven.'" I couldn't hold my breath one more minute. This was it. I had to inhale, and this was going to hurt. I could not hold my breath another second and was

3

exhausted from fighting to surface with strength I never knew I had. I was broken and beaten by the jagged walls in which I was uncontrollably spinning. I knew opening my mouth to breathe wouldn't help, but my body's survival instinct was overpowering my brain. I couldn't even tell where the surface was, it was so dark. I had to inhale, I had no control over this instinct, I just had to. I opened my mouth and inhaled as deeply as I could.

I didn't even feel the water entering my lungs; all I felt was this beautiful pure light pierce through the darkness of the waters as if God himself was reaching out His arm in the form of a brilliant warm all-encompassing beautiful soul penetrating light and pulling me out of my body by my soul.

I found myself hovering above my still fighting body, watching it spin round and round in this evil, vicious whirlpool with my head continuing to bang the jagged rock walls. I watched myself get cut and bruised and bloody, thinking why don't I feel that? Why can't I feel the pain? I continued to watch as I saw my dear friend climb up on top of my body and be able to catch a breath of air only to be pulled back down again. Then my body became completely limp' and I watched my lifeless body circle within this ferocious whirlpool, being pulled down deeper into the darkness. I watched Nancy spin round and round desperately fighting for her life. I couldn't bear it. It was all my fault. Then I turned and allowed the warm intoxicating light to draw me upward.

I could not understand what was happening to me. I wasn't hurting or cold anymore. I felt better than I had ever felt in my entire life. I felt as though I had just woken up from a horrific nightmare with a feeling of relief and comfort I could not describe in earthly words. For the first time in my life, I felt fully awake and aware of every molecule around me and its purpose in the universe. My body felt as though it had been wrapped in a warm blanket just pulled out of the dryer, alive and full of static electricity; I experienced myself as raw energy and had become unharnessed lightening.

Suddenly, I realized I had arrived at a destination, and I opened my eyes. I was first awe struck by feeling utterly and fully awake, aware, and alive. I was no longer limited by my five senses, and what I was experiencing could not be described in my mere human language. I soon realized that I was kneeling, and before me was a beautiful white cloak which radiated a brilliant pure light and raw energy so powerful that it made lightening seem dull. It was like standing in water during a lightning storm, feeling pure exhilaration. The power before me was all consuming. This power radiated from the figure before me, but the brightness was overwhelming. It took so long for me to focus. I had looked at the sun before, like most kids do out of curiosity. The sun is yellow light, but this light had no color, and it was alive and soul penetrating, pure love. It was so holy that I could not look at it. The light was love, intense, welcoming love so powerful, and I felt unworthy to receive it, so I closed my eyes.

I had not yet realized what was happening. I was far too distracted to focus on my actual location, the presence of my body in some sort of holy space. I had no pain for the first time in my life, which was fascinating considering I had not realized until then that I have spent most of my life in pain. Only the absence of it now made me aware of how I had truly suffered. I was flooded with incredible knowledge, fully cognitive of the functioning of the previously unused 90% of my brain. My "other senses" were coming to life as well. I can best describe the feeling as similar to after surgery when nerves start shocking the body as they come back to life. I was feeling these awakening shocks in good ways in my soul. My body wasn't fighting itself like on earth but was finally working in perfect harmony. I had all the answers to the hard questions I had struggled with my entire life like why children suffered abuse, cancer, neglect, etc. What's up with the dinosaurs, and why are they not mentioned in the Bible? Is God real? Is the whole Bible true? If God is real, where was He when I needed Him as a child? The list was endless, and, as I soon realized, very stupid. I now knew all the answers, and they were so obvious that I was ashamed to have even questioned.

It seemed I had been processing these thoughts for a long time when I realized I was no longer in the river; I wasn't even on

Earth. I now existed within an entirely different level far surpassing anything my human imagination could conjure. I was in heaven. That was the only plausible explanation. But I wasn't sad. How could I be this removed from my husband and children and not be sad? A moment ago, I was fighting with every fiber of my being to survive for them, begging God to live. Now I was clearly dead but feeling more alive than ever. I experienced a level of peace that I couldn't describe that reminded me of a children's song that says, "I've got the peace that passes understanding down in my heart." These lyrics are the closest expression I could relate this to and I was amazed how God had prepared me for this peace that was exceeding my expectation. A familiarity gently started coming over me that I had been here before. How could I not have remembered this place or this feeling of intense purposeful love? I was finally ready to open my eyes and try to process the radiance before me. I wanted to take it all in, knowing it was the greatest thing I had ever been close to. I knew this being only wanted to love me and was patiently waiting on me to be ready. Finally, I opened my eyes and forced myself to take in the brilliant, soul penetrating holy light.

It took a while for my eyes to focus and beyond seeing, I smelled the intoxicating aroma of God's Holy presence. This scent tickled my nose, and I could feel it going through my entire body pricking and awakening every cell in me. I had never before smelled a fragrance that I couldn't inhale deep enough. I didn't want to exhale because I never wanted to release it. This scent was multi-dimensional. It felt like my lungs were starving for more, and I craved getting enough. It wasn't merely a fragrance; it carried a powerful holy presence of truth and love and light which warmed me from the inside out. This amazing scent told a story of completely knowing and unconditionally loving me. I was experiencing an unexplainable level of joy, surrounded by His holy fragrance. When I realized I had become intoxicated by this scent, I giggled and tried to focus. I discovered I was on my knees with my head bowed. I was fascinated that I had not realized I had been kneeling. Once my eyes acclimated to the reverent glory of the light, I saw the most beautiful thing I had ever hoped to see in meeting Jesus – his perfectly pierced feet.

THE PERFECT PIERCING

To describe the feet of our Creator is something nearly impossible; how do I use earthly words to describe complete perfection? Looking upon His pierced feet was to gaze upon the most beautiful thing I'd ever seen. A glimpse of my longed-for newborn in her joyous anticipated arrival, pure and innocent, is the only earthly comparison, but multiplied times infinity. It sent such a shiver up my spine, awakening every cell in me. I was in the presence of Holiness; Jesus emanated such purity, love, generosity, and compassion. I could feel He knew every secret and truth about me, but none of that changed how intensely He loved me; I couldn't process it. He fully knew me, and fully loved me on a level my earthly mind couldn't fathom. Everything I was ever taught in Sunday school and church services about God's love for me (that I occasionally feigned interest in) was every bit true.

Seeing this big gaping hole in my Savior's feet evoked in me an incredible unsettling in my soul, a bare understanding of such selfless, sacrificial love. The Bible stories were true. This happened. It happened for me. My words are a pathetic expression of the reality of the truth that The Light of the World chose, as an act of His own will, to humbly become human, be born in a smelly dirty place, willingly choosing a life of suffering, knowing He would be tormented, bullied, and crucified, for me. Even in my then fully functioning brain that had all the answers

9

I'd spent a lifetime seeking, I couldn't grasp choosing to leave this perfect paradise for a life of rejection to save people who wouldn't ever fully appreciate it.

How can such love exist? How could I, a lifelong Christian, not have known the depths of such a pure love? I had earnestly cried at Easter services and praised God and Jesus for such an incredible sacrifice, but here, now, I was overwhelmed with the greatest desire I had ever felt, to kiss and caress these beautifully pierced feet. But I could not. In the presence of a love so great and perfect, my 5 senses were muted, I was feeling this lightening power of perfect love and comfort like a tsunami in my soul. I was struck with a reverence so great, so breathtaking, so Holy. I was not worthy to even be in the presence of such glory. I became painfully aware of my pathetic, insignificant, selfish existence. I winced and closed my eyes; it was not possible for me to process such perfection; I wasn't worthy.

Speaking to my spirit in the most loving, gentle, inviting voice, Jesus said, "See." My entire life from before birth was then shown to me in a display Hollywood's greatest producers couldn't manage. Suddenly, I was present at my parents' courtship. I was awestruck to see how I was loved and created by God long before I became a product of my parents' love and devotion to one another. Then I saw doting parents marvel as they counted my tiny fingers and toes. I saw the corrective leg braces I slept in as a baby in my crib. Also, I saw sin slowly entering my life as the light of God grew dimmer in me. I saw every lie I told and manipulation I used as a small child which only multiplied as I grew, separating me from God.

As Jesus continued showing me my life, I delighted seeing my mother come to know and choose to follow Jesus. The immediate changes in her were significant. Her love and faith spread through my family like a tidal wave. Her faith helped her stop smoking and swearing almost overnight. I was inspired by the power Jesus had to help my sweet mother change so drastically. I accepted Jesus when I was 8 years old and was baptized. I became a little evangelist briefly. I fell back into feeling sorry for myself when my asthma worsened, and I began to lose hope of Jesus wanting to heal me. It didn't take long for me to revert to choosing myself over my faith. I saw my parents doing incredible things to help my asthmatic sufferings, taking me several times daily to the hospital for shots and washing my bedroom walls daily to control my allergies. I grew to hate my parents when they put me on a crazy diet recommended by a chiropractor who claimed he could cure my severe asthma through a radical diet of herbs and bi-weekly hydro colonics. I ate spinach leaves for almost two years and took nine vitamins and supplements three times a day as my body eventually became too weak to attend school, and I became bedbound, spending my days in bed waiting to die. I was reduced to sneaking out of my room at night and foraging for crumbs under our dining room table or from the trash can, angry and starving.

I saw my parents choosing to move to Oregon after the doctor insisted my parents take me to Arizona where the dry heat could perhaps give me a chance at living. That's when I became a rebellious selfish teenager and ended up in juvenile hall for four days at age 13 because I refused to submit to authority. Seeing this evoked the worst pain for my parents, and I watched my mother sobbing and my father trying desperately to console her as they fervently prayed that God would help me in spite of my selfish rebellion. Sadly, I continued in sin as a runaway for the next four years, living lie after lie to manipulate others into housing me. I wanted to punish my parents for trying to control me; no one could control me. I was consumed with deep self-pity and selfishness, but why? Seeing this in heaven at the finish line, my choices were obviously childish and dumb. Why didn't I see that when living it?

As I walked through the shame and guilt of my life, I became sickened in my spirit. The word shame only began to define how disgusted I was by my own choices. My soul wanted to vomit. I then viewed myself interacting with boys, wanting so desperately to be loved and saved from myself. I did horrible things to get inappropriate attention from boys who could care less about me.

11

I saw one of my teachers reacting to my destructive behaviors telling me, "You're white trash Whende; you'll never amount to anything. You'll be a drain on society all your life." This only evoked more hate and rebellion. I was unstoppable at that point. I hated myself so much I stopped caring what happened to me. I saw myself beaten, abandoned, and half naked on a rural street seven miles from home. Blood ran down my legs, and my nose was broken. It was hailing, and I was horrified someone might see me. I fell to my knees, pounding with both fists on the street screaming at God, "If you're real, where are you? How could you let me suffer like this? Don't you see me? Don't you care? Why did You even create me? Am I just entertainment to you? If you are real you better come rescue me right now, or you better kill me because I'm done. I can't live like this anymore, save me or take me." God was silent.

Next, I watched myself being raped in consequence of more of my stupid choices. I saw myself climbing out of bathroom windows to escape, too ashamed to tell anyone. I saw the embarrassment of that trigger more self-destruction. At this point, all I could think about was suicide. I wanted desperately to be loved. I cried out to God again. I begged Him for a man who would love me, and I promised to live for God if He would just deliver me from myself through another person who would care for me. I saw myself trying to be a better person and even becoming liked by many people, but still hating myself. I watched myself making lists for God in what I wanted in a spouse and writing what I would do if He blessed me with this person. I wrote my promises to serve God and raise babies to love Jesus at the bottom of this contract I was trying to get God to honor. I begged God to allow me to realize he was "the one" when I met him. I then saw myself meeting my husband. God made him appear radioactive like he was glowing. It was obvious this man, Tony, was "the one" the moment I met him. God blessed me by giving me what I prayed for, but in my brokenness, I began manipulating Tony to love me and chose me rather than trusting God and His timing. I saw myself struggling through challenge

12

after challenge because I would not trust or wait on God's timing.

I watched myself getting married at 19 years old and living on food stamps and in poverty because I wanted things my way. I watched us bring our first child Tegan into the world; she was another perfect undeserved miracle in my life, and I gave her to God as I promised, but not really. Instead of praising God for my perfectly healthy baby, I repeatedly threw God in my husband's face, blaming my husband for our struggles. If only he were the spiritual leader I needed him to be surely God would bless us. I saw myself throwing around the word divorce like it was confetti at a party. Instead of trusting God, I saw myself wasting countless hours thinking about the men I should have married, who surely would have treated me better. I saw myself pregnant for the second time and repeating the vain attempts to be loved unconditionally. All the while I subconsciously cursed my husband for his unemployment, even though he suffered from a broken back. I cringed seeing myself in hard labor as the doctor told me that if I didn't sign the forms in agreement to have my tubes tied, he wouldn't perform the prearranged cesarean I needed. I heard him telling the nurses I was "white trash" and his taxes were paying for my welfare children. I heard him threaten to fire them if they helped me in any way. I watched a nurse cry and be comforted by a fellow surgical nurse before I passed out. I woke up two days later with a disfiguring scar and a beautiful baby girl who I gave to God, but not really. I heard myself preach at my husband and others with arrogance and judgement only driving them and myself further from God.

Moving forward through my life, I saw myself working with children at a large church, telling myself I was a woman of God, when really, I was just going through the motions. I was only serving myself and trying to convince the world I wasn't "white trash Whende" anymore, instead, a woman of God with perfect children, so I set unrealistic expectations on my husband and children to be perfect.

When I had my third child, my son Austin, God performed another huge miracle. Austin had to be delivered prematurely as

13

he barely had a heartbeat, and he was so big that my incision from my previous delivery was tearing open. My husband was working out of town. I was rushed into surgery for an emergency cesarean, grateful that my mother was with me. Austin was born blue and unresponsive. My mother's heartbroken expression told me what I couldn't see. She stroked my hair and cried as we both started crying out to God. We asked God to breathe life into my baby boy, and after seven minutes of intense prayer, my son took a breath. He didn't breathe again for three minutes but we never stopped praying. Finally, he was breathing. God saved my son. We were only in the hospital briefly even though Austin was in ICU for five days. Watching God save my son again reminded me of all of the promises to God that I failed to keep. Jesus lovingly showed me throughout my life how I was so arrogant and self-righteous. I was often asking God to take my husband, to kill him, because I felt I deserved something better, yet I couldn't bear the thought of him with another woman. Due to troubles in our marriage, my husband was not present when my son was born. Meanwhile, I continued to work at the church and live a life that looked to others as though I had it all, but my actions were not for the Lord. They were all to prove to the world that I was no longer "white trash Whende." Shortly after the birth of my son, I realized I could no longer work outside of my home as my son (now six months old) had special needs due to his lack of oxygenation at birth. My husband built a Christian preschool and daycare center for me. Thomas Learning Center (T.L.C.) is where I met my friend and client who I convinced to go rafting that day. For the next two years, I continued to live a fake, prideful life of lies. I pretended to act as a representative of God when serving my own agenda. Jesus showed me my entire disgusting existence, living so far from truth.

Through this visual journey I realized I had achieved a broken and wasted life. I was appalled by the choices I had made while taking the effortless way at all the crossroads of my life. Often it was to prevent hurt feelings of others, but mostly it was out of laziness or selfishness. In this vision, I realized countless

14

opportunities to be like Jesus in showing love to others, but I didn't notice them because I was too busy focusing on myself to look up and outside me.

My life was a revolving series of lost lessons as I was only talking to God and never listening, constantly looking in the mirror, rather than looking to God. Now I was at the feet of my Savior and aware of my wasteful life. I'd been an actor, playing a role of a woman of God, a wife, and a mother. I had faked my faith for approval, not because I loved God's people but because I wanted them to love me. Now on my knees mesmerized by the big beautiful hole in my Savior's feet, I was painfully aware of what perfect sacrificial love looked like. How could I live with myself for all eternity, knowing my earthly life was the opposite of what it should have been?

FIRE

"But who can endure the day of his coming? Who can stand when he appears? For he will be like a refiner's fire or a launderer's soap. He will sit as a refiner and purifier of silver; he will purify the Levites and refine them like gold and silver. Then the Lord will have men who will bring offerings in righteousness." Malachi 3:2-3 NIV

These few simple verses carry incredible weight. I wish I could tell you that meeting our "Refiner" was a cake walk, and perhaps for you, it will be. For me, however, it was far from easy. I wasn't in the least bit concerned before I died about the "refining" process. I was a woman of faith, loved by many, kind to most, serving God daily in my Christian preschool and daycare. I was a faithful wife and mother who thanked God daily for my blessings. I raised my babies in church and brought people to the Lord. I had all my bases covered. I really had turned my life around before heaven, and I confidently believed I was a good person.

I would have liked to have told you that on my arrival to heaven God excitedly met me at the Pearly Gates with a red carpet welcome, high-five, a big hug, and congratulating me on a job well done. That He had presented me with my eternal treasures that I'd been certain I had accumulated, maybe a tickertape parade or a few thousand confetti cannons and at least multitudes of angels ushering me in with song, but that's far from what my experience with the Lord was.

When I saw Him, I truly could not stand. The scripture that says, "No one can stand in His presence" is an understatement. I was kneeling at these beautifully pierced feet unable to stop crying. I was trembling with shame and self-loathing when again my Father spoke to my soul and said, "See." Jesus again showed me my life but this time through His eyes. I was instantly overwhelmed with a love and happiness that I can't fully explain. I could feel the love Jesus had for me, like I was His masterpiece, exactly who He created me to be. I was giddy to experience my story through His eyes, surely this wouldn't be as painful as the last replay. This time I saw where He was in my entire life story. This was a separate complete vision of my life; I was seeing myself through the eyes of the One who loved me enough to die for me. His intense love and compassion for me was intoxicating. It was the greatest gift I'd ever received. Knowing how much precise attention was put into creating me was so inspiring. For the first time ever, I finally felt "beautifully and wonderfully made."

He showed me how, throughout my entire life, the Light of the World had been right by my side. From before I was born, He had created me and had been delighted in me. From my birth and transition into this human world, He was with me. In my early childhood when I was left alone and scared in the old cage like cribs in hospitals, sometimes being there for weeks, He was with me. Throughout my childhood battling severe asthma, fearful each painful breath would be my last, My God was holding me. During my childhood full of countless nights sitting up, unable to sleep, fighting for every breath and terrified I'd never wake up, God was there giving me the strength to breathe.

I was again shown my baptism but seeing myself come into faith through Jesus eyes was very different. It was so powerful, this celebratory love. I saw all of heaven rejoice with me for choosing Jesus. He was so proud of my choice, and it was indescribable how grateful I was to give Jesus that feeling. I giggled watching Him delight in me; He danced with joy in that season of my life. I couldn't believe my salvation meant so much to Jesus, I never felt so special and cherished as I did seeing the wave of joy my salvation caused in heaven. It was then that I first noticed a vapor like crown of gold appear on my head.

Again, I saw myself slowly grow away from God; it broke my heart feeling Jesus' sadness that I wasn't stewarding the fire He put in me. Throughout the crazy diet the chiropractor put me on, I was certain I would starve to death. (More than once I'd taken food from a garbage can at home or school to satisfy my hunger.) I was too weak to do much of anything but hate everyone for allowing me to slowly starve to death, saying it was for my benefit. Yet my God was there, sustaining me constantly. I saw Jesus frequently helping me swallow the handfuls of pills. He was up with me on all those sleepless nights, comforting me and giving me the strength to fight for every painful breath. Loving me with such tender compassion, despite my anger and self-pity, He never left my side.

I saw myself about eleven years old, hiding in my closet listening to my parents argue with my grandfather in the adjoining room. My grandfather had wanted my parents to take me to Arizona for the dry climate. The doctors had strongly advised this plan of action to get me out of the Los Angeles smog and to give me my greatest chance at survival, but my parents felt God wanted us in Oregon. My grandfather claimed the Oregon climate would kill me; my parents said I was likely to die no matter where they lived. The day I heard them arguing with my Grandfather was a dramatic turning point in my life. I again saw them saying it was time for them to focus on my little sister, who'd been neglected due to my severe health problems. I decided that day my family thought I was only an expensive inconvenience. Jesus then showed me how I had only heard just part of the story which made my choices throughout my teen years seem asinine. My parents weren't moving to Oregon, so I'd die faster; they were following God's will. I had completely misunderstood them.

God showed me how from that point on as I continued to

make horrible choices, certain I was unloved and unwanted, Jesus was there protecting me from myself. The Creator of everything, from the universe to the atom, never left my side. I had lived a very destructive life from then on, certain nobody cared. Failing countless classes to punish my parents, my life of lies and self-destruction led to loosing many people I truly cared about, but never God. I had even given up on myself; I hated myself, but the Creator of everything loved me fiercely and had never left my side.

I again saw myself on Roller Coaster Road, beaten and bloody, standing alone in the rain, soaked and half naked. I was crying out to God, but this time as I saw myself cursing Him, but He was beside me and holding me and gently loving me, whispering in my ear that He was there and promised to never leave me or forsake me. He kept the cars away as I trudged that road, protecting me from being further humiliated. If cars would come, He provided a deep ditch to hide in, and as I hid in the culverts of wet muck, He was right there holding me, crying with me; my pain (although self-inflicted) also caused Jesus pain. He grieved with me through every bit of my suffering.

God showed me how He orchestrated the people in my life at pivotal points to keep pointing me to Him. When I was at my lowest, God was there, and everything I thought was a happy coincidence was my God's calculated handiwork. Even being locked up in juvenile hall was God's protection as I had planned to kill myself that weekend. I cried out to God many times in my solitary confinement cell, "Please kill me God. I want to be with you. I can't bear this." I remember feeling abandoned yet again and so painfully alone. God was there, and now I was seeing how I had chosen to be a victim. I should have felt His warmth as He held me so close, but instead I chose to feel sorry for myself. The time I was crying in my cell, I was actually being held by my Creator. My severe asthma attack in lockup surely should have killed me. Only I was foolish enough to run away on a four-day weekend when there was no judge to write medication orders. I fought for each and every breath, counting them like minutes, but

God was there, allowing me just enough pain to be sure I wouldn't repeat this stupid mistake again. I watched as He lovingly held me through my suffering, tearful over my self-destruction.

The dark emptiness of juvey brought about change and so did getting put back to the eighth grade halfway through my freshman year of high school in a different school but the same small town. It was then I decided no one could fix me but me. I needed to become someone I could love. I watched as God strategically placed peers in my life who were making better choices that I respected. I watched God create such a confidence in me as I joined with those who were making the good choices. My life became easier. Although I was still struggling with authority, God consistently put people in my life who kept pointing me toward Him.

God showed me how He had placed a kind Christian woman, whom I lovingly called Aunt Billie, in my life. She lived exactly far enough from my home that by the time I reached her house after my frequent running away, I had calmed down, stopped shouting obscenities, and had run out of steam. He showed me how that if she had not been there, I would have gone into town and made even worse choices. Aunt Billie had always opened her door to me, fed me, and prayed for me. She took me to church several times and out to breakfast after. She even drove me to youth activities far away, so that I could see how peers who loved God behaved. God gave me Aunt Billie at that perfect location and time in my life.

I did not go to church regularly through high school, but I did pray frequently. I was too cool to show it, but I could feel God's presence during many close calls. This helped me become more likable and confident. It was necessary since I was constantly putting myself in stupid situations. I spent countless nights walking home after games on scary, unlit, dark country roads, hiding in swampy, cold ditch culverts to escape a trucker who often tried to rape me. Yet God was there as I heard that trucker call out and search for me, promising he just wanted to give me a ride, and God kept me hidden. I was terrified because I was wheezing so loudly from running to hide when I saw his logging truck coming towards me on the dark highway. I felt as though my heart was beating so loudly that if the trucker didn't hear my wheezing, he'd surely hear my pounding heart. But God was there with me again in the muddy culverts. God showed me how the quick intuition He gave me saved me from other possible injuries and emotional scars. I was never alone. I chose not to feel God's presence because acknowledging it would mean I had to stop being a victim.

I saw myself again lonely by my senior year of high school even though I had lived with my best friend (a Christian) off and on for years. God showed me provisions I was unaware of through high school, but by far Jennifer was my greatest. Through Jen, God saved me from myself. She challenged me to not be a slacker. We changed the spellings of our first names as an act of rebellion, but for me it was because I wanted the world to know I was changing. I didn't want to be white trash Wendy; I wanted to be better. Jen's character and actions amazed me. As a teenager, she helped maintain her parents' adult foster home and worked and studied hard; she even maintained Honor Roll, all amidst her parents' divorce. Jen never let herself become a victim. During this time, I mooched off her and was little to no help because I was too busy having my pity party. God showed me how He gave her and her family such undeserved patience and compassion for me. It's obvious to me now, that clearly it was God through Jen because anyone else would have kicked me out.

Then I saw myself again crying out to God to give me a man to love me, and all the while God was there. Seeing myself through His eyes, I was completely consumed with adoration and compassion for my young self. Nothing I ever experienced on earth could compare to this pure devotion my Father had for me. However, in heaven we are not limited by five senses. There I received everything at a frequency my human brain didn't perceive. The closest comparison is that upon entering heaven, I finally felt fully awake and alive, unlike the dream state I was in here on earth. It was like going from black and white static TV to high definition 4d color IMAX theater quality.

I smiled as I watched my young self pleading with God to bring me my husband to rescue me from my loneliness and make me feel valued. Jesus then showed me how He lovingly created my husband Tony. I delighted seeing Tony's childhood, including all the struggles Tony endured to make him the perfect other piece of my soul. God showed me that it was long before I asked God for my soulmate that God had strategically engineered Tony to be my other half. Then God gave me the gift of seeing Tony, and how I met him for the first time on November second of my senior year. God showed me that He had allowed our struggles as a newlywed couple to make our bond stronger. God showed me the gifts of my healthy girls Tegan and Teryn, coming into the world, finally bringing me the gift of love I had always ached for.

I saw myself crying out to God when my son Austin James Thomas was born dead. I then saw God breathe life into my baby, and my son came back to life. This was yet another miracle in which I neglected to give God the glory He deserved. This had been a lifelong theme for me: The Lord giveth and I walketh away.

I now had two beautiful daughters and a miracle son, and with them the thing I had wanted most in life, unconditional love. I had everything I ever wanted: beautiful home, handsome husband, and beautiful babies. Why did I not show greater appreciation to my God for fulfilling my dreams? I became so wrapped up in myself that I'd forgotten to sincerely count and celebrate my rich blessings. Throughout all of my ingratitude, I was being lovingly held by my God who made these miracles happen.

Then Jesus showed me how although I claimed to give my babies to Him, I was constantly taking my children away from Him. I prayed my babies would grow up to be warriors for Jesus, but at the first sign of them facing a battle, I was begging him to stop all their suffering. I begged Him to give them all their wants (although they were ridiculously spoiled) and prayed He would heal all their sufferings But, how can a person become a warrior if they've never seen battle? It was embarrassing to see God working in their lives as I had prayed He would do, only to see myself complain and get angry when they faced turmoil or challenges.

It was painfully obvious to me that I had wasted my life choosing to be a selfish, vain victim. My life had been a series of tests and challenges to develop me into a strong woman who would someday truly serve God, even though my entire life I had treated him like an ATM by only going to Him when I wanted something.

I was horrified and disgusted when Jesus showed me what I had done in an effort to steward my many blessings. Expensive gifts I'd insisted on buying for my kids that were thrown away months later. My life was so petty; I had a spirit of wanting. Always just one more thing I needed to find happiness, but God is a father, why would He continue to bless me with so much when I didn't take care of it or appreciate it? At the feet of my Father I was shown the amount of garbage I'd created in my 28 years before I met Jesus. Every time I see pictures online, of the island of trash, I am reminded of this. God gave me a beautiful planet to steward, and in return, I gave him a mountain of garbage.

But my island of garbage was not as offensive to God as my arrogant judgement of other people. God showed me how much of my time was wasted, spent on judging those who offended or hurt me when that time could have been spent in praise or worship of my King. My judgement didn't stop at those who offended me; my judgement even was over other religions. I truly thought if somebody was in a different brand of Christianity than I was, they weren't going to heaven. I was so ashamed of myself when I saw how this grieved my Savior. We who believe in Jesus are supposed to be on the same team.

Jesus showed me the amount of selfishly wasted time I had spent thinking of ways God should punish others for hurting me or those I cared about. I often prayed He would punish people and even suggested how He do it. He was amused by my stubborn self-pity, like we are when we see a dog chasing its tail in circles for hours with such commitment. You know that when the dog finally gets a bite of its tail, it's going to hurt. But the dog continues to chase his tail in hopes of finally getting a taste. I'd spent my whole life trying to catch my stupid tail. Yet, I brought Him joy even as I was building a wall of sin between myself and God. My wall was something the Chinese would pay to come see. The Great Wall of Whende, the eighth wonder of the world. Fortunately for me, what I saw next was greater than any earthly wonder.

THE TRUEST SERVANT

The Good Book tells us, "How beautiful are the feet of the one who brings the good news." Those words never prepared me for the magnitude of reverence I would feel. I was on my knees at the beautiful feet of Jesus, feeling so joyful yet ashamed of my hollow wasted life. Then my Lord showed me such a tremendous gift, the entire earthly life of Jesus.

I saw the Father, Son, and Holy Spirit preparing to send Jesus into our evil dark world. I've always thought of Jesus' sacrifice as unimaginably painful, but God had to show His love in the most significant way. I would much rather be tortured than watch my child suffer. I believe there's no greater pain than feeling helpless when someone you love suffers unjustly. All of heaven grieved but respected what Jesus chose. The pain of just being separated from heaven and the Father's presence and aroma, I truly don't believe anyone would choose to leave heaven willingly, but Jesus did. He choose to step out into darkness for us.

I saw Mary, a young woman, chosen to host the Son of God in her innocent, pure virgin body. I watched as she prayed over her unborn child not herself, concerned for his life and not her own. I saw her question why God would choose her, thinking she wasn't worthy of such an honor; I marveled at how the Holy Spirit worked in her as well as Joseph throughout her pregnancy, as our King chose to enter this world in such a humble manner.

I marveled at the sinless life of Jesus happening before me. I was seeing the most spectacular story unfold in 4D, no glasses required. Watching Jesus' life was incredible as He hungered to learn scripture and obsessed over drawing closer to His Father in heaven. His life was about service and gaining wisdom. While He sought to know as much about His Father as He could, He was chastised for being different, but He never let it change Him. He had a mission, and nothing stood in His way. During His whole life on earth, He remained humble, kind, persistent. Jesus pursued His Father's words with intense passion and in complete obedience.

I watched Him being baptized by John, further displaying His humble nature. All of heaven celebrated when it opened, and the Holy Spirit poured over Him, anointing His prophetic journey. I looked as Satan desperately tormented Him in the desert. Jesus was so hungry and tired but stood honorably against evil, even at His humanly weakest point.

Jesus, then as human as me, performed countless miracles. His compassion was constant, always putting others first. His kind, gentle, patient demeanor was like a mysterious magnet drawing people to Himself. These miracles were not performed to gain fame or favor but to win souls for eternity.

I ached as I saw Jesus devastated that the temple was turned into a marketplace, and the ones pledged to uphold His Father's laws profiting with arrogant self-righteousness as they turned this holy place into a business.

He loved children; He delighted in their honest innocence and curiosity. He loved people, all people, like they were all His Father's children despite their sin. He radiated that love every single day of His life. The Bible covers the highlights of Jesus life, but to walk through each day with him was wondrous.

I saw demons tremble and retreat in fear of the Son's name, Jesus. I loved seeing them hide in the dark places only to be revealed by my Father's soul penetrating light. They knew the very mention of the name Jesus would result in their suffering. Their very existence was a desperate attempt to take us from our Father and to drag us into darkness where we could fulfill our sinful desires, to get us to focus only on ourselves. The more time dwelling on the sinful desires, the greater the wall of darkness becomes and the stronger our deception. This gentle, loving, humble man, was an undefeatable warrior to a pathetic army of demons. None could or would stand against Jesus except Satan, and even he wasn't capable of making my Jesus stumble.

I ached in my spirit as I saw Jesus pour His pure unreciprocated love out over so many people in His lifetime. They came to him in droves always wanting healing, cleansing, or just to feel hope. They had the Lamb of God in their presence and could only desire more from Him, and Jesus gave and gave and gave. All Jesus asked was that they believe and turn from sin. This seemed a fair enough exchange but was quickly forgotten by most. They would praise God momentarily and then slip back into lives of hollow selfish gain. They treated God's Son, our only hope, as if He were a genie in a bottle, and He loved them anyway.

Seeing Jesus ride into Jerusalem, being treated with such reverence, filled me with awe. He heard their praise, but He knew it wouldn't be long and He would be sacrificed by many of these same people. Yet, He never let that change His love for them. He was in constant communication with His Father praying that God would forgive what these people were about to do to Him for the joy set before Him. Towards the end of Jesus' life, He didn't stop in His constant communication with His Father. He knew what was coming. He knew it would hurt, and He knew it had to happen; it was the only way to save humanity from itself.

I was fascinated as I watched my Jesus prepare for His own death. He knew what was to come, and yet He loved so selflessly. He chose to make memories for His followers and bring them joy by loving them, all while His death was looming. In His mind, He was scared and never let it show. He celebrated His last supper with the men He loved, and though He knew they would deny and fail Him, He washed their feet anyways and prayed for their courage for what was to come.

He taught them how to partake of His body and blood, so they would be able to teach and remind countless generations to come that this happened for me and for you. He knew His minutes were a precious few, and still He chose to give us sinful, selfish, arrogant humans a way to remember and celebrate His love and sacrifice for us. He broke the bread, knowing His body would soon suffer such devastating physical pain. He gave them His body to consume, and because of our sin, His body had to be destroyed. Yet He wasn't resenting us; He was praying for us. He chose to be grateful as He poured out the wine representing His blood that would soon be spilled, for He would be with His Father soon.

When Judas betrayed Jesus with a kiss, Jesus loved him. When the soldier's ear was cut off, Jesus compassionately healed him. Knowing He was about to die, He was still thinking of others. When beaten and mocked, He was thinking of us. He had the ability to end the suffering, but He chose to endure it. He chose to feel every excruciating tear of His flesh as they tore handfuls of His beard out. Jesus looked deep into my eyes as I was sobbing desperately, begging Him to make them stop. He said to me, "I choose you." I couldn't swallow; I couldn't breathe. I couldn't move. If I were the only sinner on Earth, He'd do it just for me. Nobody's ever loved me like that, and I was powerless to stop His pain and humiliation. My Savior was exhausted, spit upon, and taunted by His very own children, but He wasn't judging them, only praying His Father God would have mercy on them.

I watched sobbing as Jesus walked in agony toward Calvary. I couldn't stand what I was seeing, but I knew my pain was a miniscule fraction of what Jesus endured, so I forced myself to watch. It was the least I could do; I didn't want to see this. I wanted to carry His cross. I wanted to bear His sufferings, but my sacrifice couldn't amount to anything, for my life was not one of purity and honor, but of selfishness and excuses. Only Jesus could bear this cross, and He wanted to. I saw His prayer, His constant communication with the Father, focused not on Himself, but only His mission: to live and die and live again, to bring glory to His Father.

As the nails pierced him, excruciating pain consumed His flesh and His spirit, yet He never lost sight of His purpose. Hanging on that cross as the crowds mocked Him was much like His sufferings in the desert, being tormented by Satan. He could have stopped His sufferings both times. Instead, He chose to feel every bit of it. As the nails were being driven into His feet, I was acutely aware of my sins, the reason for the pain Jesus was enduring.

At the cross, I saw myself in every person there: the mocker, the laugher, the soldiers, even the ones hammering the nails. I saw myself in each one of them and knew He loved me, and prayed for God to forgive me. It seemed forever before Jesus drew His last breath, and I was only watching, agonizing over my part in the crucifixion of my King.

Next, I saw the heavens celebrate as Jesus fulfilled His purpose; finally, it was over. I saw Jesus rise again three days later fulfilling His prophecy, "Destroy the temple and in three days I will raise it again." I loved seeing His friends' faces when they realized it was Jesus. He arose just as He promised, igniting their faith. They loved hearing him speak, and they couldn't wait to serve as the body of Christ, a church, to show everybody that Jesus really is the Son of God, resurrected as the perfect Lamb of God.

Once back in heaven, I was overwhelmed with gratitude for the sacrifices of the Trinity. I was thrilled that in my lifetime I had chosen Jesus and was now with Him in heaven. However, it felt a bit like when on a road trip and one arrives at the destination and realizes, "I don't remember the drive." In heaven my life felt the same way. God had given me spiritual gifts like He has given to each one of us, but how had I used them to serve him? Could I have truly spent the last 28 years of my life just going through the motions like an actor on a stage? What did I have to show for my 28 years as a woman of faith? I'll tell you what, a whole lot of Whende.

Because my efforts in serving God were largely in vain, my treasures were all on earth. My ministry, my children, my marriage were all behind me. I had lived an empty life. My meaningful

31

connections had been shallow, and my faith had been knee-deep. My self-indulgence, however, was as powerful as the river that ironically took me to the feet of Jesus. I was ashamed, humbled, and so overwhelmingly grateful. I looked up, trying to gaze into Jesus's eyes so He could see my gratitude, but still I couldn't. That quickly changed when He so lovingly and gently lifted my chin.

HE DELIGHTS IN ME

Seeing myself through the eyes of my Savior was certainly the greatest gift I'd ever received. After what Jesus did on the cross for me, I was basking in His perfect endless love, marinating in God's infinite grace. I was celebrating that my race was finished; I had won. Everything made perfect sense. It was a brilliantly orchestrated plan that I was a small piece of, and all my suffering was finally over; I made it to heaven. At Jesus' feet I had every need, physically, emotionally, spiritually, filled. Beyond my utmost desires, I was completely and deeply loved.

As I remained at Jesus' feet, He gently lifted my chin and showed me my reflection in His eyes. I was wearing a golden crown and I was beautiful; I was young, and I had a glistening long vapor like veil that seemed alive coming from my crown. My sparkling veil followed me, floating as if on a wind. I started to dance around spinning like a child to watch it twirl. It was about six to eight feet long, a vapor-like cape flowing behind me. Jesus spoke to my soul explaining that the glittery particles were rare gems, and that the veil held my music, which was my identity, telling my life story on earth. The gems in my veil created the music. I was mesmerized by my music; I could see and touch gentile vibrations that tickled my fingers. Jesus showed me what my acts on earth amounted to in eternal value by what was happening on the cape fluttering behind. Each time I had shown love or truly honored God, precious colored gems appeared on the cape depending on how generous my loving deed was. If I had been kind when others were cruel to me or I had put others before myself, a small lovely gem would appear but almost transparently on the cape. Some gems were the size of my hand and others the size of a coin or glitter.

As I became prideful and arrogant and judgmental of others, the gems evaporated in a single moment. Now on my knees at His feet, I realized that my pride had caused any eternal rewards to vanish. I reached back to the veil hoping that some gems remained but could not see anything but the radiance of Jesus' holiness. Jesus then spoke to my soul, "I have nothing for you child because you were not serving Me but only yourself. You were so busy looking in the mirror that you were not looking up." Saddened by His words, I knew them to be true. The thrilling music of His presence was still with me, but I had cheated myself out of my eternal treasures. Never-the-less, at the feet of Jesus, I could not stay sad after seeing the intense passion the Father took in creating, protecting, and loving me. I realized I had far more than I could ever want or need, and I was finally home, experiencing a love that felt like an all-consuming intimacy.

I'm going to try to not cheapen the feeling of being in the presence of Jesus. I will simply say there is only one human feeling on earth that can almost begin to describe the feeling of being in heaven. It only occurs during intimacy. How fitting that the most intimate moment of my existence felt like that on steroids times infinity.

Jesus then said, "See," and He motioned to the right. On a small pillar was a large book with light and energy radiating from it. Within the light were twinkly little flecks of radiating life-giving energy very similar to the light that carries our music and eternal rewards that follow us in heaven. Jesus opened the book and the light became too brilliant to look at, and it took a moment for me to regain my sight enough to focus on the words written on the page. Engraved were the names of my father, my mother, my husband, myself, and my three children. I then realized Jesus was showing me The Book of Life, and my family's names were in it.

There's no sense of linear time in heaven; therefore, in the blink of an eye my entire family would be here with me. I was ecstatic upon seeing this, and I buried my head in Jesus' robe and wept unapologetically without restraint for this perfect gift.

Jesus then spoke again, and in one simple sentence everything changed. He said, "You must go back." Instantly, my emotions turned from complete joy and thankfulness to that of a terrified child being torn from her mother's arms. I cried out to Jesus begging Him not to send me away, clinging to His robes unwilling to let go. Jesus spoke again, "You must go back." I just couldn't let go of this perfect place filled with the intoxicating aroma of God's love. I begged frantically, twisting my fists around in His robe as I was being pulled away from Him. I pleaded and promised everything I could think of. "Please Father, don't make me go back! I can't do it. I can't leave you. Why can't I stay? Please Jesus, don't send me back, I won't leave you." I was gently and carefully pulled from my Father by an unseen force.

Without warning, I was back in the frigid river. In an instant, I had gone from perfect soul penetrating warmth and comfort to bitter bone chilling water and pain. I was back against my will and separated from my Savior, my safety, my everything. I frantically fought to drown under the water. I wanted to die. I couldn't stand the thought of being away from Jesus. An angel pushed me from the darkest depths of the river up onto a rock ledge. Devastated, I had no control over leaving and was given no explanation. Suddenly, I was back in the darkness of this sin filled world with a completely broken heart. How could I go on? I no longer had all the answers; instead, nothing made sense. I started screaming, and He responded with silence.

EIGHTY – SIXED

The river had spit me out onto this rock ledge, and I was back in this nightmare. This world which I once found so beautiful now felt disgusting. I was separated from my God, and I could no longer sense His warmth or feel His insatiable love. The river I found myself in is a picturesque place, boasting of God's beautiful artistry. At this moment, however, it felt like I'd been dunked in the bowels of a state fair port-a-potty on a sweltering 100-degree day on the last day of the fair.

I couldn't see my friend Nancy anywhere, and my self-pity quickly turned to panic as I realized my friend, who I had convinced to join me, had been swallowed by the hungry river. My eyes combed the river's edge, but she was nowhere to be seen. I had just killed my poor innocent friend. Not only was Nancy gone, but our life jackets and oars hadn't surfaced either. I began screaming frantically for Nancy, pounding on the rock wall as if I could force her to surface by showing God my anger.

Within seconds, I saw my brother and sister coming down the drop in their raft. I was so relieved. They were alive. They miraculously had navigated the plummet which had been hell bent on consuming us. As they rescued me from my ledge, I couldn't speak. Internally, I was fervently begging God for Nancy to be alive. I was certain she was dead. I was certain she didn't survive this river's rage.

We rounded a small bend in the river to find Nancy alive and only shaken on the river edge. I was ecstatic, and I couldn't contain my grateful tears. I still, though, couldn't speak in complete sentences. I couldn't process this profound experience. I had been to heaven. Who would believe that? But I wasn't allowed to stay.... why? Don't I get a reason for having to leave? I felt like a child finally getting to go to Disneyland, getting to ride the train around the park and seeing its adventures from afar, and then having to leave without ever actually entering and enjoying the rides. Was this a cruel joke? How could I express this experience with my floating buddies? I have always been the jokester of the group, so they'll never believe me. Because of my silence and sadness, they grew concerned, so I told them finally:

"I died, and I went to heaven ......I was with Jesus."

Despite the raging river and the joy of our reunion, our raft was quiet. They could tell I meant it., but I just cradled myself in the fetal position and cried. I wanted to get home immediately and write down everything I had seen. I needed to be alone with God to cry out to Him. I'd certainly never heard of anyone seeing heaven and living to tell about it. I didn't even believe that was possible. But in the last hour so much of what I had always believed had forever changed.

The river was rushing rapidly, but time seemed to drag. Nancy and I were in my raft, both terrified and traumatized by what we'd each encountered. I couldn't look into Nancy's eyes; I was so ashamed. We finally reached a slow enough spot in the river where we could pull out. We were all thrilled to be off the river. As we walked, I could focus on nothing but my experience with Jesus. My brain hurt; I just needed a good cry and a long nap. I didn't have the strength or the energy to figure this out. My body was in a significant amount of pain, but it paled by feeling rejected by God.

When I returned home, I immediately went to my room and started writing. I couldn't put down my pen; I had to write down everything I had seen and experienced in heaven before it all melted away. The tears rolled down my face faster than I could dry them, splattering the words on my page. I was certain if I documented my experience, the very moment I finished, God would take me back home to heaven. I poured out every bit as feverishly as I could. I convinced myself I was just back here briefly, as if on a work visa from heaven to let my family know I was leaving. I had seen their names in the Book of Life, so in the blink of an eye they'd all be there with me. I was just back to tell them, "Don't waste your life stressing over the challenges and heartaches of this world. This world is temporary. Heaven is forever, and it's the opposite of this."

As I struggled to write, I wondered how my children ages two, three, and six would be able to grasp my experience. My husband, whose faith was shallow, came into the room to ask me about my day, and I just looked at him with contempt. Perhaps the reason I was forced back to this life was because without me my little children would not grow up believing and loving or serving God. Then I began to think this was all my husband's fault. In my confused and angry heart, I despised my wonderful husband – I just couldn't speak to him; I could only cry. My brother and sister then came in to see how I was, and they explained to Tony that I had died, and I was angry that God wouldn't let me stay in heaven. Confused and angry, Tony looked at me with such pain in his eyes. I suddenly felt badly, knowing he was hurt, but there was no way to explain to him that I was no longer the same person after spending ten minutes in heaven. I still couldn't speak, so I just kept writing in my journal. My family would read my story, and they'd surely celebrate me being finally and forever safe, and as soon as God took me back, completely loved.

My brother-in-law and sister convinced Tony to get me to the hospital immediately. They got me there somehow, but I was too busy writing to notice. Before I knew it, I was in a gown getting crammed into a tube for a CAT scan. My doctor was trying to take my journal from me, but I refused to let him. He was a family friend, so I wasn't as compliant as I typically would be. He said, "Whende you can't have that in my machine. You'll blow us all up." I replied, "I'm not done writing. I met Jesus today, and I know that sounds crazy, I don't care. I have to write down every detail, so I'll never forget." He then lovingly took my journal from my grasp and gently stroked my head to comfort me. His attitude completely changed. He knew I was telling the truth, and he leaned down and whispered in my ear, "Don't worry, you won't ever forget. I promise. They never do." I was shocked by his statement. I thought, "Wait a minute, what? You mean I'm not the first? There have been others who've met Jesus.... and didn't get to stay? How is this possible? Sure, now there are books and movies about heaven, but my experience was on Memorial Day of 1996, and this kind of experience was rarely told. Could it be true? Others have come back from heaven?"

My test results came in, and I was going to be fine, severe concussion and a few minor lesions/bleeds on my brain. I was bruised and beaten but had suffered no permanent damage...yet permanent change. I vaguely remember my family being there at the ER. My life after was a blur. I don't remember much about this world that afternoon.

MELANCHOLY & DISAPPOINTMENT

My dear friend Angie called in the afternoon to hear about my day, and I told her I had the best/worst day of my life. I couldn't understand it. I'd gone to heaven, and I think I had gotten kicked out. My friend wasn't a Christian, yet she believed me. She showed up seemingly minutes later with a beautiful card and pizza. It was a great validation. She believed that I believed I'd met Jesus. Would the rest of the world? She knew better than most what a flakey, jokester person I was, but she recognized I was telling the truth. Maybe my husband could understand as he was getting deeply offended that I wasn't sharing my journey with him.

I finally yielded to his grumbling and told him briefly, "Babe, I went to heaven...IT'S REAL." He looked at me as if I were severely brain damaged. He seemed fearfully concerned that I could believe such a thing. He asked, "So... what's it like?" with a smirk. I was so upset, I felt he was patronizing me, so I replied with something truthful, but super hurtful to him. "It was incredible, the best thing I've ever experienced." He seemed entertained by my seeming delusions. After all, I was starting to think it was his shallow faith that forced me back here. I decided he didn't deserve to hear more. So, I decided to wrap the conversation up with a harsh truth. I told him, "You don't get it; if God took all three of our kids to heaven tomorrow, I'd be ok." His jaw dropped. My poor husband looked at me with disgust like I was a monster. How could any mother say such a thing? Perhaps you're thinking the same thing. Trying to define my experience was like endeavoring to explain color to a blind person or make a deaf person understand the beauty of an extraordinary musical composition.

My husband insisted that I not tell anyone my story because he was sure others would think I was crazy. I angrily refused to keep my heaven experience quiet because for the first time in my life I knew truth. However, I finally agreed to keep heaven to myself after he pointed out it would hurt our kids to be known as the kids with the crazy mom in our small town of less than 300 people. Knowing his reasoning, I submitted to his will, but not discussing my experience only created a greater resentment toward my husband, and a huge struggle emotionally that eventually manifested in me physically.

Before heaven, I couldn't make myself cry. I'd bring a needle or stick a thumbtack in my thighs at funerals trying to make myself cry. I didn't want people to know I was dead inside. But after I died, I couldn't seem to stop crying and feeling. I'd cry over Hallmark commercials; I'd cry and almost lactate over starving children commercials. What was going on? Getting kicked out of heaven turned me into an emotional wreck.

I pulled back from my many children's ministries at the small church where I worked since I was too emotional. I was dying to share my story but knew folks would think I was crazy. I tried my best to go on as nothing had happened, but I couldn't trust myself to keep silent. I was the duck, appearing to smoothly glide across the water, but under water, I was frantically scrambling just trying to stay afloat. Although I had many memory blanks, my husband and children remember me being distant and irritable. Suffering deep depression, I was sure that God knew I didn't have the intelligence to figure this out on my own since my gifting wasn't intellect; it was being a professional victim. My oldest daughter Tegan remembers me napping entire weekends away after my death. She was clearly the most affected of my children. Because Tegan was the oldest, I had to teach her how to help run a household. I knew God wasn't cruel enough to send me away for more than a year, so I had to get my children as self-reliant as possible. When God brought me back to heaven, they would be a blessing to their new stepmother. Tegan knew my story and, although I didn't speak it verbally, my smart daughter knew that I didn't want to be here. How tragic for a seven-year-old to see her mother want so badly to leave. I just knew God would give my children a much better mother, and my husband a much better wife. My husband believed I'd lost my marbles and considered leaving me several times if only to protect our children. I'm so grateful to God that He didn't. I'm certain that next time I get to meet Jesus, I will see some very fancy footwork on His part that kept my family together.

Our small town was separated by the river that took me to heaven. I had to take my kids to school every day, crossing the river where I died. I couldn't drive over any bridge for years without crying and feeling abandoned by God.

As time went on, I started accepting that I may be stuck here for a while, but why? Perhaps I was going to have to share my heaven story publicly someday when my kids were older and wouldn't be ridiculed for my beliefs. If He wanted me to share the reality of heaven to get people prepared, my life had to change. I could not continue ignorantly as I did before heaven. My motives in serving God had to be authentic, but I didn't know how fake I was until I was at the feet of Jesus. How could I know I was doing things for God and not as a manipulation to serve myself? I decided the only way I could make this happen was getting to know God on the deepest most intimate level like Jesus did. I had to pray, study, and memorize as much of my Father's truths as possible. I had a perfect blueprint of what I needed to do; therefore, I simply needed to figure out how to die to my old self and resurrect who I was created to be. It would be the only way out of my melancholy and disappointment.

ADVENTURES IN ALZHEIMER'S

Shortly after my death, God performed a miracle, and my family moved into a house that I had been praying about for over seventeen years. I also moved my Christian daycare/preschool to Mill City, Oregon. It was a dream come true. For years I'd taken my bus of kids to play at a park across the river from this historic home. I'd rest at a picnic table between pushing my little angels on the swings. I'd pray God would someday bless me with that house. My daycare kids knew my dream and would often pray with me. Now through pure miracles, I had my dream home. The only thing between my park prayer table and me now was the river that delivered me to God.

Within months of buying my dream home, we discovered that my husband's great uncle had severe dementia. I cherished this precious man who never married but cared for his mother dying of cancer for 40 years. He was a humble and gentle man of God, and a Veteran – two of my favorites. I convinced my husband we had to care for him. The nursing homes he could afford were bad. He deserved to be loved and doted on.

Elvin Lester Marlow moved in with us in our new home in 2002. He was wonderful with my daycare kids. He enjoyed them. Senior Services required me to become a certified federal caregiver to host uncle, and soon after, they insisted I choose between my Christian daycare business or uncle. How do I stop teaching these sweet babies about Jesus? Uncle already knew

Jesus and even with severe dementia, he could almost recite the entire Bible. Uncle had sacrificially served others for Jesus his entire life, and I was tormented having to choose, so we prayed as a family. My new home was two hours from my husband's job. He was already grumpy about the move, so losing my income wasn't an option to him. I trusted God was wanting me to care for Uncle. So, I closed my lucrative business to care for a man who couldn't remember who I was or whose house he was in or urinate without a catheter. My husband was right, I was crazy.

The big day finally came, and we moved a senile sweetheart into our home. The next eight years were a circus of uncle's public nudity, his urinating in the artificial trees in Costco, and firing and locking the kids out of the house for being the worst cooks and housekeepers he'd ever had. He often woke us up around 1 am, by pulling hard on our hair. We'd wake up terrified and shouting, uncle dear would just chuckle and say, "Oh thank God it's still attached, I thought the headhunters gotcha." With a relief he'd laugh gently the whole way back to his bed. Uncle Elvin, however, was an incredible blessing. During the next eight years of almost being shut ins, I had abundant time to process my heavenly hall pass. I had to come to terms that perhaps I wasn't going to go back to Jesus, at least for a while.

Looking back on that long hard season, I now see all that my children learned through our taking uncle into our home, so much more than any educational system could teach. All three of my kids at one point or another had to look after him. Each one of my kids changed his diaper at some point, or bathed him, and cooked for him. We didn't ask them to; they just loved him and served him well while I was out running errands. He never knew our names, insisted we were trespassers in his home, and sometimes he became aggressive. But Elvin remembered scripture and was the kindest, most gentle, appreciative man I've known. He began most of his stories with, "A little birdie told me," and most of his stories ended with, "I can tell by looking at you, you're the one who ate all my groceries." Poor uncle was always hungry. I loved cooking for him all day, and although he

46

thought I was his hired help, he was so grateful for all my efforts for him.

Through His incontinence, we learned patience and compassion. Through his public nudity and blowing his nose without tissue on the floor in the middle of Taco Bell, we learned humility. Uncle never knowing our names, taught us perseverance. Uncle trying to microwave or boil our cat, taught us to be more attentive to the needs of others. Uncle, thinking I was a fat and ugly kind madam at a whorehouse, taught us how to laugh at ourselves. When the police brought him home at three in the morning after he'd snuck out to go hunting through the snow in search of a band aid. Being brought home bloody, barefoot, and half frozen, we learned the value of a bed alarm. All our adventures with Uncle Elvin distracted me from my depression which had been growing by the day. I now realize having Uncle Elvin in our home gave me a best friend I could tell all about heaven without fear of his judgement. I was in a safe space where my secrets of heaven could be verbally processed. Uncle even backed up my stories with scripture references which made me hopeful that I really had gone to heaven.

I often asked God why He sent me back if He wasn't going to use me? Uncle knew God, my kids were saved, why was I sent away? I just continued to pray for answers while feeling I was selfishly subjecting my family to a crazy life. What if I was wrong for choosing Uncle over my career? Why couldn't I hear God's voice? Every day it was the same: diapers, catheters, chaos and kids. I felt overwhelmed being responsible for a husband, three children, two birds, dogs, cats and a crazy old man who rarely slept, and who constantly accused us of stealing his car. (His license expired in 1983, and he moved in with us in 2002.) My husband was growing bitter. I was doing a poor job of making him my priority, and he was traveling four hours a day for our family, all so that I could live in my dream home. One day he became really grumpy and said, "I guess I'm going to have to sh** my pants to get any attention around here."

I was growing more and more disappointed in myself. Every

night I'd lie in bed and pray and feel sorry for myself, going through my checklist with God. "Took care of Tony, took care of the kids, spoiled uncle, took care of the household, served and honored God. I accomplished all you've given me. I'm exhausted, and ready. Please bring me home." I prayed this for over eight years with no response.

In May of 2008, my brother-in-law Michael was killed on his motorcycle. A week later a dear friend suddenly died, and just after that my precious Uncle Elvin died. All three wanted to live, but God took them. I wanted to die but was left here. I couldn't bear these losses all at once. Then, shortly after the loss of Uncle Elvin, I was faced with having to tell my husband our savings was gone. Caring for uncle's medical needs had consumed our savings. My hardworking man, who drove four hours a day, so I could live on the river (my peace, or stairway to heaven) deserved so much better. I was ashamed of spending my husband's hard-earned money on Uncle Elvin's medical bills. I had to fix this problem I'd put our family in. I decided I must go back to work. My oldest was engaged, and I had to help provide her the wedding my husband and I never had. I was too emotional to go back to work with children at this point, so I decided I'd find an easy temporary retail work position.

My frustration with God's silence in my life was at an all-time high. I was desperately homesick for heaven, and this one-sided communication was draining. "I'll do whatever you ask, Father; just tell me. This can't be your will for me. Changing diapers? This is my great purpose? Is this my only asset to you? My wiping abilities?" I constantly cried out for answers as the light grew dimmer and dimmer the longer I was away from heaven. I was drowning again, my mind spiraling, pulling me deeper into darkness.

FROM ONION RINGS TO ANSWERS

I felt alone the day I went job hunting. How was I going to serve God and fulfill my destiny for him working retail? However, I felt I had no choice as I wanted my daughter Tegan to have a beautiful wedding. I got on my knees and cried out to heaven, "Why was I sent back? I am getting tired of treading water, and I need answers." I sobbed while getting up from my knees. God was quiet.

I hopped in my car and headed for Salem and Keizer to drop off resumes, praying I could control my emotions enough to not look like a crybaby-lunatic to the store managers I would meet. I was able to fake a smile through the last drop off. I was hungry, but the only money I had was the change in my ashtray. I knew that onion rings from Burger King would help my tearful heart. I got in the drive thru line and placed my order. Immediately after I ordered, my son called me on my cell phone. I tried to sound happy and asked how his first day of high school was. He replied, "Awesome mom, I love it. Could you buy me some colored pencils on your way home? I have a project due tomorrow, and I have to have colored pencils." I explained that I had just spent my last bit of change on onion rings. I didn't have money for pencils, but there were crayons in my desk he could use. He retorted, "Thanks a lot mom. You definitely need onion rings more than I need to not look like a baby." Then he hung up on me. Once again, my selfishness had hurt my family. I was sickened by my gluttony; when I got to the take-out window, I couldn't control my tears. I paid for my onion rings and started for home. By the time I got on the highway, the smell of the onion rings that were sure to brighten my day were now a nauseating reminder of my love for self.

I was furious with God as I drove down I-5, "You know what Lord; I must have brain damage. I didn't really go to heaven. Because the Jesus I met was far too loving to allow me to suffer like this. I must have dreamed my whole heaven encounter. If you love me, You'll Speak to me now." Silence again. "You are pissing me off bigtime Lord. How about you come down here and prove to me you're real, that I really went to heaven. That you actually give a sh*t about me? Because, right now I'm calling bulls#.t on everything I thought I saw in heaven. It couldn't have really happened. I must have dreamed up the whole thing, or have brain damage, or you've just chosen to forsake me. So, what is it big guy? I don't believe the Jesus I met in heaven, would force me to suffer this B.S., so what's it going to be Father? I want answers." I was flipping heaven off through my sunroof, yelling and sobbing at the Maker of the universe, trying to force a face to face conversation.

I must have entertained countless drivers that day, but my anger was raw, and my heart was broken. I didn't want to live another moment. Then I pulled onto the off ramp to wait at the stop light. There on the corner sitting on an upside-down bucket was the cutest homeless person I'd ever seen. He had bright white hair and beard and wore clean blue overalls. He looked just like Santa Claus. I couldn't help but laugh when I saw his cardboard sign. It was a cute drawing of Mickey Mouse pinching Minnie Mouse's bottom, and Minnie was slapping Mickey's face. The sign read; "YOU THINK YOU'RE HAVING A BAD DAY?" I started to laugh through my tears. The man saw me and motioned for me to roll down my window. Reluctantly, I did. I felt awful not having any money to offer him.

He said hello with a sweet smile, and I interrupted with an apology. "I'm so sorry honey. I have no money for you today. I wish I did." He smiled even bigger and winked his twinkling eye at me and asked, "What makes you think I wanted something from you?" I responded, "Well, you're here...on the corner... with a sign." He laughed and corrected my observation by saying, "I don't want anything from you. I want to give you something." Now I smiled and asked with a smirk, "What could you possibly have to give me?" His sweet face grew sad as he asked, "You think I have nothing to offer the world?" I realized how arrogant my words sounded and apologized. I quickly explained that I was having a very bad day and begged his forgiveness. I asked what he'd like to give me. He smiled again and said, "I'd like to give you my colored pencils." He then reached into his sack and pulled out a bundle of colored pencils rubber banded together. He said, "They're good quality, and I don't need them anymore. They've served their purpose because they made you smile." I was shocked. How could this kind little man know I needed colored pencils? I realized my mouth was hanging open like a fool when he chuckled, enjoying my shock. His eyes twinkled with joy as he added, "Please take them. I know you need them." I asked him with a trembling voice, "Hum, how do you know I need them?" He again chuckled and replied with a wink, "A little birdie told me," and then my heart flew wide open. How I missed those words my sweet Uncle Elvin used to tell me countless times a day. I said, "I'm sorry, I can't take anything from you." He looked sincerely hurt by my words. He insisted, "Please don't deny me the gift of giving," so I reached out and took his precious gift. I suddenly realized I had onion rings I could give this sweet man, and I insisted he take my onion rings, but he stopped me and said, "Oh, and I have something else for you – a message. Our Lord, the maker of heaven and earth wants you to continue doing exactly what you're doing. He so delights in you." I couldn't breathe. In a state of confusion, I again tried handing him the onion rings, but again, he gently refused. The stop light turned green, and he nodded to me and added. "Enjoy your onion rings sweetheart. You deserve them."

I pulled away with colored pencils in hand. Three minutes ago,

I was at my lowest, raging in frustration to God, and now I was soaring. I had cried out to God daily for answers since I was kicked out of heaven; for years I had constantly grieved Jesus for not answering my cries. Could I have really just gotten a message from the maker of heaven and earth, from a guy with a cardboard sign at an intersection? Was he an angel?

In a three-minute stoplight my world was changed. My Father answered my selfish, childish tantrum with His gentle loving compassion. Surely, I couldn't have been as annoying as the arrogant Israelites for whom God performed countless miracles, even parted the Red Sea. Could I have been wandering the dessert in my own life, starving for direction because of my own attitude? I realized I had handed Satan the keys to my spirit and let him drive me right back into self-pity and grumbling against my Father. It was right then and there that I took back the keys. My attitude was mine to control. I was done being a victim. I found myself standing in a field about a mile away from that stoplight. I'd been pacing and trying to process what it all meant, not realizing I'd pulled over in front of the state prison. I must have been a sight for the officers in the tower who were probably watching my every move. I didn't care because I was so excited to finally have my answer. My heaven experience was real; it happened.

I needed to call my husband to tell him what had just happened. He would be coming up to that very same intersection any minute. I was excited when he answered, and he kept having to tell me to slow down because he couldn't understand a word I was saying. After all, I was standing beside a busy interstate in a penitentiary field bawling and ecstatic that I had just encountered an angel.

I cleared my throat and slowly repeated, "Honey where are you? I just met an angel sitting on a bucket on the corner of I-5 and Hwy 22 off ramp. He gave me colored pencils. Please give him $20.00 I had no money left because we're broke. He gave me a message from God. I really did go to heaven. I didn't know how to tell you I spent our entire savings on uncle's medical bills. He might really be a homeless man, so give him all of your cash, please. I'll explain everything when I get home."

Tony finally responded, "Did you say we're broke?" He clearly wasn't understanding how happy he should be. I had just had my life changed. He repeated, "Babe, did you say we're broke, and you want me to give all my cash to a bum on a bucket?" Why did he seem so confused? For the first time since heaven I wasn't confused.

He said, "Just wait a second. I'm pulling off on that off ramp now, and Babe there's no bum here. Nobody is at this off ramp."

The fact that my chubby little guy was gone cemented in me the fact that my Lord, again, went to extraordinary lengths to get my attention. This time I wouldn't keep it to myself.

I couldn't get over why God chose me, an uneducated perfectly average sinner, to share this message, but I knew one thing for certain. I was done asking why. I know He's perfect, and His plans are like a beautiful symphony, every note connected. From that moment on, I had a purpose to constantly praise God. I would share my story with anyone who would listen.

FAITH IS AN ACTION VERB

I finally had my answers. The void in my aching heart was filled, and my life was about to change in more ways than I could imagine.

I had come out of Spencer's Hole telling my closest friends I believed I just met Jesus, and I had been in heaven, but I guarded my reputation by sharing with only those closest to me. Now, I told anyone who would listen. My attitude was a 180° transformation. I was on fire. I no longer cared if people thought I was crazy. That was between them and Jesus. I had wasted the last 13 years trying to live for God while internally having a pity party for myself.

My encounter with that precious man on a bucket reminded me of the deep feelings of hopelessness I had once wallowed in. How could I have been delivered to such incredible blessedness and still be such a victim? I often taught of the Israelites who were delivered from incredible suffering, shown incredible miracles, and still cursed God. Like them, I'd been delivered and given proof of the reality of God and heaven only to jump right back into my patterns of arrogance. How could I show God I wouldn't spend another second in self-pity but would forever joyfully serve Him?

I was moved by my stop light miracle. Regardless if he was a homeless person or an angel, I knew my orphan spirit could help others who are going through homelessness and feeling devalued.

I remember being homeless through high school and terrified my friends would know. What if I could show those suffering the same way I had, how God delivered me and changed my life? I could show them love without judgement and see their worth as a child of God.

I started making a list of what things would have meant the most to me as a homeless runaway. I soon came up with such an extensive list that a small bag wouldn't contain them all, so I decided to start with a backpack. I'd fill every fold and pocket with a surprise. This became my first ministry. I had been a teenage runaway who felt unloved and forgotten by God. As a transition into my first real ministry, I took new or used backpacks and filled them with necessities like a flashlight, hotel soaps, shampoos, a blanket, deodorant, and gloves, McDonald's gift cards, and a Bible with highlighted verses that helped me through the tough times.

I wrote a heartfelt message on the inside cover of the Bible explaining that Jesus changed my life, and I now knew first hand that He is real, and every word in the Bible was true. I'd promise to pray for them and ask them to please pray for me. I know from when I was homeless it was heartbreaking not being able to show my gratitude by giving back to those who had helped me. Asking the homeless or afflicted to pray for me allowed them to give back and feel self-worth.

I would keep these backpacks in my car to give at intersections where I saw the homeless holding signs, but I much preferred giving them out when I took warm or cold drinks, depending on the season, and cupcakes to the parks where the homeless gathered. Listening to the homeless and sharing my story of healing and redemption and being able to pray for them and love on them through laughter and hugs is what filled my homesick-for-heaven heart. Before long, I grew accustomed to sharing my testimony with people at checkouts or gas pumps.

I couldn't help but think of how I had failed God in countless ways, from treating Him like an ATM to only serving when it benefited me. I had lived the first half of my life focused on me, and I was desperate now to serve God for all the right reasons. I knew I was saved by His grace; I'd seen my name in the book of life. I wasn't trying to earn anything through my serving God. I stopped praying God would take me home and started begging Him for just another day to serve Jesus.

There Are No Mirrors in Heaven

I don't believe there are mirrors in heaven. I know from my brief time there, our concerns in God's kingdom are on love and joy, not self. Heaven celebrates God's intricate artistry in everybody, a perfect place where God's opinion is all that matters. We will celebrate our differences in heaven inside the beauty of knowing our Father loves us each enough to create us with thoughtful and purposeful lives. Each of us is uniquely wonderful and a piece of the puzzle that when whole, becomes the perfect body of Christ. It is what has been broken in each of us that makes room to fit into this puzzle. We are exactly who God created us to be, made in His image.

I had developed my homeless ministry, but still I had an aching in my spirit. My life was far from a living testimony of my time in heaven. I had been shown at the feet of Jesus what my life could look like if only I had used the talents He gave me to serve Him.

One such talent, and in my opinion by far the most embarrassing, turned into a ministry at my pool in my backyard. I profoundly love children of all ages, and they love me. In our small town, we did not have many healthy choices of activities for the children to do. I was blessed to offer children a place to swim during the summer, but in Oregon that's only a small

YOU MUST GO BACK

window of time, so I started an undercover youth group and never told the members it was youth group. I simply preached in a way they didn't know I was preaching. For example, I decided to drain and open my pool to the kids to skateboard during the colder seasons. This proved a big challenge because my old pool had a tiled topless mermaid inlaid in the center. How could I have a ministry with my hoochi-mama mermaid, affectionately named "CORLENE," perkily greeting my guests? I put some seashells stickers on her bosom and prayed it wouldn't be an issue; fortunately, it never was.

The kids loved coming to skate in my pool, and I was honored they loved being in my home. My husband had no idea I allowed this. He was always concerned with being sued, but I knew God would protect my ministry. In the year 2004, saggy pants were the ridiculous trend, and I'd insist my young guests pull up their pants, but they'd insist it was part of their "gangsta" identity. A few of my precious thugs claimed they weren't going to college after high school but were going to become professional rappers. I'd indulge their dreams by offering to pay for their studio time if they could rap-battle me and win, but if they lost, they would need to pull up their britches and focus on an education. I have a secret love of rap music. I won't say I'm proud of it, but I can truly relate to it. I was also a preschool teacher for most of my adult life, so Dr. Seuss is my homie, and I can rhyme almost anything. But why rhyme anything when I could rhyme Biblical truths. I battled many of my dear thugs, and I never lost. Thus I developed my next ministry.

One of the sweet young men was arrested several years later, and many times I drove five hours one way to see him in jail. The punks he was locked up with reminded me of my own young thugs at my pool. Many were dreaming of becoming famous rappers and being in jail gave them "street cred." I started battling them under the same conditions, and again I didn't lose. They would line up to battle me in the cafeteria of the jail. One family day, my husband joined me, and we were visiting with my young man while an extensive line of boys were patiently waiting to hear

60

or battle me. My husband was becoming uncomfortable with these thugs lined up and staring at me. I laughingly asked him what was wrong. He said, "I think those boys are trying to get your attention." I just smiled and said, "Yes, they want to rap battle me." He was shocked and assumed I was kidding. So, I waved the group over. Tony was scared to death I'd embarrass him, and he quickly got up and walked away acting as if he didn't know me. My husband watched from across the room as the Lord gave me words to biblically win over each of these precious young men. Before I was done, my husband was back sitting at our table, impressed with my silly gifting. A bit later a handsome boy and his father approached me apologizing for missing my battles. The father was an attractive black man in a beautiful business suit with gorgeous dreadlocks halfway down his back. He introduced himself explaining he was a local rap music producer, and his son was an upcoming rap star. He asked could I please battle his son because the prison staff had insisted he hear me. I embarrassingly agreed. The son looked as uncomfortable as I was when I started with a simple verse, "Step to me son, let me seal your faith, when I'm done with you, you're gonna wanna cuddle your cellmate." His son just stood there speechless with his mouth wide open. He finally spoke and said, "Dad how can I battle her? She's an old granny?" His father handed me his business card and offered to represent my career as the Rappin' Granny. I politely refused his offer.

Although I'm often embarrassed by this gift, I've been told by numerous children that they don't understand the Bible but would listen to me rap scripture all day. I'm still fine tuning my gift. Once my story is made public, I may move onto celebrating this gift. This will only happen if I constantly remind myself: There are no mirrors in heaven; it's not about me being embarrassed but about giving God's message to those who might not hear it otherwise.

SMALL SACRIFICES = BIG BLESSINGS

I was finally emotionally well and ready to start using my gifts to serve my Savior. I desperately missed teaching preschool, but I knew if I was going to teach children again, I would need a greater focus and a mission. Because I wanted to build warriors for Jesus, I wanted to not just pray over them, but to pour into children all that I had learned in heaven. I had a fervent desire to get back into teaching ASAP.

I got on my knees and poured out my heart to my Father. I knew this drive could only be powered by Him, so I readied my heart and asked Him to make my path straight. I was being considered for my dream job as a Children's Ministries Director at a Salvation Army Center. This entailed overseeing the preschool and daycare and other children's activities. I would be able to encourage hundreds of children to love Jesus. The office and salary were just a bonus. I'd arrived, and God was going to bless me with my dream job. In my mind, I saw him putting the pieces beautifully together to honor my efforts.

I met a new friend at Garden Club who was a pastor; I loved her, and we became fast friends. She and her husband shepherded a small humble church in my little hometown. She shared with me that she felt God wanted me to start a preschool at her tiny church. I assured her I felt God wanted to put me in my dream job. After all, He did kick me out of heaven, so I deserved this. After really thinking and praying about it, I became aware that if I got what I deserved, I'd be falling in fire for all eternity. I had already been given so much and I needed to get over myself. When I sought if this was God's will for me, I felt warm and tingly, and I assumed it was a confirmation from God. When I opened my eyes to get off my knees after praying, I saw a beautiful beam of light coming through my bedroom window. The ray of light seemed alive with tiny floating dust particles, and I was awestruck at how it powerfully reminded me of my Garment of Glory in heaven. I was thrilled knowing God was reminding me how my sacrificial loving service for Him earns great eternal rewards.

I joyfully opened a tiny preschool in my little mountain community. I daily prayed over my babies intently and taught them to recognize their spiritual gifts and use them to serve the Lord. I helped them memorize over 40 scriptures and biblical truths throughout the school year. I taught those children many things, but I learned far more in that season. I learned everything from why urinals are only for potty (something I learned the hard way) to how children's minds are so much greater than adults.

One day after sharing my heaven secrets with my little cherubs, one of my precious boys asked, "Teacher, did God let you pick out your own wings in heaven, so you could fly around like a butterfly?" I quickly indulged his thought by making photocopies of a wingless angel and asking my students to draw the wings they would choose if given a choice in heaven. I marveled as they discussed their choices and reasoning. Some wanted Bumble Bees' (from Terminators) wings, so they'd fly the highest and the fastest. Others wanted butterfly wings, so they'd be beautiful. I wanted ladybug wings because I love red and polka dots, but my choice was very concerning to one student. I asked him what was wrong, and he gently responded, "Teacher, please don't pick ladybug wings; you should pick big jet plane wings because you're really chubby, and I want to fly fast with you in heaven."

A year of teaching seemed to fly by, and then I received a call at the church by a member of Medical Teams International. He

64

asked if our church would host a Dental Van to donate free dental care to the uninsured people in our community. I had been praying over a friend's teeth for years, and I was thrilled to help. Without even thinking about it, I developed my dental van ministry. I found this hilarious as I hadn't seen the dentist in 20 years. I continue to help local people with dental pain find relief. They contact me by social media, and I pray over them and get them the resources they need. I also share my story of heaven with all the folks needing help. We try to host the Dental Van twice a year.

I loved this precious church and had started more than just a preschool ministry in my time there. I also started a Sunday School, a Bible Study (for middle school aged kids), and a special club for girls only. Our small town had an abundance of girls growing up without fathers in their homes. I saw many young girls seeking unhealthy attention from boys, and many were depressed, self-harming, and suicidal. I couldn't bear seeing these girls going down the same dark path I'd traveled. I opened my pool weekly to these middle school girls for a lunch, support, and prayer time. I'd tell a brief Bible story, and we'd apply it in our lives. We'd list our goals for the summer, spiritually and otherwise, and we'd hold ourselves accountable all summer long. I'd always have another adult assisting for liability reasons. I'd feed the girls piles of food, and then we'd swim and play while listening to Christian music. I was able to teach the girls that Jesus was the only perfect Father, and He was always with them, loving them. No boy would ever love them the way Jesus would, and no friend would ever listen to them like Jesus would. I constantly pointed them to the only One who could rescue them through everything. By the end of summer, the girls were so close and supportive of one another. I encouraged each girl to discover and develop the spiritual gifts God had given them to serve Him. Many of these amazing young women served with me in our annual Vacation Bible School.

Through this season of juggling many ministries, I grew to develop a love for serving. I couldn't get enough of these blessings, and I finally felt I was living authentically as a woman of God, though nowhere near who I wanted to be, but far from who I once was.

Is Prophecy Still a Thing?

Soon after developing nine ministries in 2015, I was approached by a stranger one day when visiting my daughter at work. He claimed he had a message from God for me. He put his hand on my shoulder and said, "I'm going to give you a word of knowledge." I was intrigued for two reasons. First, this black man clearly loved the Lord, and he claimed that Jesus and he chatted together. Second, I'd never heard of a word of knowledge. He explained he had a message for me from God, and the word of knowledge was simply a fact that he would have no way of knowing about me other than hearing directly from the Lord. He asked if he could share this message with me. I was excited and doubtful he would know anything special about me. I remember at the time thinking, "I finally get to make a new black friend, and he's nuts. Thanks Lord." I smirked, trying to hide my mental diagnosis of him and told him to please continue.

He shared, "God is showing me that you work with small children. You teach them, but you're much more than a teacher. You're building warriors for Jesus. You pour your heart into these kids, custom fitting their spiritual Armor of God." I had just told my husband the day before, "I'm building soldiers in The Lord's Army." This stranger had my complete attention. He continued to tell me the Lord's message. As I listened, I became astonished. I didn't know something like this was possible because in my conservative religious upbringing I never saw this.

I tried my best to listen and retain all that he told me as I prayed for wisdom and discernment. (I was just waiting for him to bust out a crystal ball or some Tarot cards.) He told me, "God is showing me that He is driving a chariot, and you're the horse pulling Him. You keep fighting His guidance charging into battles that aren't yours while He has a clear and easy path for you, but you're fighting the reins and His will. You're exhausting yourself because you're avoiding the easy road by not letting God guide you. The battles are your ministries. He's given you several warnings. If you don't stop your ministries and let go of what your clinging to, He will make you let go, and it will hurt. God delights in you in a powerful way. God loves your servant's heart, and He is making a way for you; it's time to tell your story."

Shocked, I interrupted him, "Do you know my story?" He said, "No." Then he continued, "Your story will bring so many people to the Lord. Many more people than you can imagine will hear it and be changed. Not thousands, or tens of thousands, but millions. That must be why God shows me you're covered with gold glitter. Jesus delights in you in the most beautiful way; you make him so happy He dances. You carry a very rarely seen, but huge, Holy Spirit presence." I thought this man had lost his mind. How could he be so right about me building warriors for Christ, but be completely wrong about me? I'm nobody. I'm just a redeemed sinner with a cool story, and I'm certainly no preacher. I thanked him for his message and walked away perplexed.

I then met my daughter who told me a woman had given her an invitation to a church evening service, insisting that God said my daughter and I should both attend. We thought we might as well check it out. After arriving at the service, I immediately became very uncomfortable. This once conservative was surrounded by people as crazy on fire for Jesus as I was, and it freaked me out. I had heard Pentecostals were wild, so I'd cautiously avoided them my entire life. Nervous, I wanted to bolt, but I was feeling the Holy Spirit powerfully moving in me. One lady during worship started dancing with silk flags. My daughter and I just looked at each other waiting for the other to make a

IS PROPHECY STILL A THING

run for the exit. Just then this flag dancer came over to us and tried to hand me her flags. She explained the Lord wanted to see me dance with her flags and worship him. Clearly this woman was unaware that I was way too cool to dance with flags in front of strangers. I like to think that I carry the Fonz anointing, so I'm way too cool to dance like a Jesus hippie. I smiled as I gently shoved her flags back at her and kindly insisted that if Jesus wanted me to dance for Him, He was going to need to come tell me that Himself.

I was further shocked to see the black man who had recently given me the message from God at this service. My daughter and I listened as he gave a clearly anointed teaching. He didn't even remember meeting me when my daughter and I went up for prayer. Once he realized he had met and prophesied over me, he chuckled and started praying in tongues over me. I felt my hands and feet getting warm then hot and tingly as this man put his hands on my head and poured out his anointing on me. The mere fact that my daughter and I allowed this to happen was a miracle. Our comfort zone was totally breached, but we both felt the Holy Spirit, so we just let it happen. This man of God, I now know as Tim, started giving my daughter Teryn a message that was incredibly accurate, and we still laugh about it. After he prophesied over us, others started to further comfort and encourage us. He again emphasized that I needed to stop all of my ministries and tell my story to the world. He also said again if I didn't obey God's message and let go, it was going to hurt. The people at the church service around me all agreed with this man. They heard God saying the same things. They assured me I'd just received a prophetic word from God and all wanted to hear my story. This prophet Tim did say God delights in me, and I'd heard that in heaven and from my homeless man/angel. When I returned home that night, I was perplexed and intrigued. I got on my knees and begged God to reveal what I was holding on to and refusing to let go of.

Within a few months, I realized my ministries at the church were what I couldn't give up. I loved my precious little church.

The people of this church greatly loved Jesus, and I loved serving there, but I felt I was becoming unappreciated by a few church leaders. I had recently asked for prayer from the men-only elders meeting that I unwittingly interrupted one Sunday morning. I desperately wanted to be prayed over by my leaders since I was struggling with a Wiccan group who was trying to coerce members of our youth group into witchcraft. I loved all these children, so I needed to respond with love, and I desired spiritual backup from my peers. I quickly and nervously explained that I could really use prayer, and my direct authority elder asked me to get the devil's tongue out of the church. I quickly explained I knew God had my back, but I needed to be careful, so I could win these children to Christ, but I was asked to be quiet. In this church women were not often encouraged to speak. I was reminded by that same elder that in 1 Corinthians 14:34, "Women should remain silent in the churches. They are not allowed to speak, but must be in submission, as the law says." I left this meeting feeling defeated. Soon God showed me the church was what I was clinging to and that I had to let go. He taught me the hard way what happens when you don't listen to His warnings.

God called me away from teaching after a few years. It hurt deeply as I had ignored God's gentle warnings. The prophet was right. God had given me a powerful story and rather than risk looking like a crazy person, claiming I'd been to heaven and sharing Gods truth, I was hiding behind my many ministries.

That season taught me so many valuable lessons, and it also reminded me of what I had learned in heaven. We are to listen carefully always. When we hear the same thing twice, God is clearing His throat to get our attention. When we hear the same thing three times, God is shouting, and we must respond immediately because if we don't, when we hear it the fourth time, it's going to hurt. It sounds harsh, but I know God isn't unjust. He wants us to learn to hear and obey His voice.

I now knew prophecy was still a thing as there was no possible way any of the strangers I had recently met would know any of the things they told me unless God had told them. I had some investigating to do. Fortunately, after raising many kids, I had become a skilled detective.

RED FLAGS TO A RED MOTORCYCLE

My friend Tim, who had already spoken truth over my life, heard my story of heaven at a healing service a mutual friend hosted for His Love Heals Ministries. He again spoke over me, telling me God delighted in me. He asked me to be a guest on his local talk show called Hope and Healing with Timmy Chatman. I was excited for this opportunity but was terrified by the thought of representing God's story. I had allowed my weight to get out of control because I had done my best to eat myself to death to teach God a lesson for casting me out of heaven. My new friend Tim was so kind to support me by having me as a guest on his show. It felt great to finally publicly tell my story. After seeing and hearing myself on his show, I became physically ill. My face was so fat you could hardly understand me, and I looked like a chubby elf who lived in a tree and baked and ate cookies all day. My body was more like the Pillsbury Doughboy than a temple. I had destroyed God's temple. Upon realizing that once again I'd fallen into arrogance and victim mentality, I couldn't bear to look at myself.

I was heavily convicted how once again my rebellious nature had hurt my ability to represent heaven. I began begging my husband to let me go to Tijuana, Mexico to have a gastric sleeve surgery. He refused because all the people we know who've undergone weight loss surgery are now divorced. He said he would rather have me fat and happy than skinny and single. The thought of surgery in Mexico was also terrifying to him, but I wasn't the least bit concerned. I knew what I was put here to do, and God had a plan for me, so I felt bulletproof. I pleaded, and Tony persistently refused. I went to the local training and information classes at our hospital but wasn't willing to spend the ridiculous costs of a copay when I knew I could do it for a fraction of the cost in Mexico. I prayed fervently God would change my husband's heart. I had needed my knees replaced for over a decade, but with a BMI of 49% it wasn't even an option. As a result, I could barely walk, and I lived on pain medication. I was afraid to speak at events because the required standing for extended periods of time hurt and caused me to shake like an addict. To avoid this, I'd have to take enough pain meds that I wouldn't be able to focus on telling my story. I was told by God to end my ministries and tell my story, but I couldn't even form a complete sentence. Again, I cried out to God this time to end the vicious cycle of pain medication and lack of focus. When I went for my initial knee replacement consultation, my surgeon agreed my knees should have been replaced a decade ago, but because I was so heavy, no insurance would cover the risk of surgery. My doctor said it was unlikely I would ever get them replaced because nobody gets to weigh almost 300 lbs. without trying to destroy their body. I told him that day I would be back in a year for my surgical date setting appointment. His words motivated me powerfully. He was right. I had to cry out to God for my next steps.

For me, crying out to God looks like me on my knees, and hands to the heavens, worshiping in song and praying loudly. I typically do this as soon as I roll out of bed. I sing:

"Good morning God,

This is Your day.

I am Your child,

Show me Your way."

I learned this song while volunteering in the children's program at Bible Study Fellowship. It's so simple, but it's my heart song. It reminds me that no matter how old I am, I'm a child of God.

God answered my prayers through a miracle. Tony's friend stopped by his shop one day and shared how he lost well over a hundred pounds very quickly. He was a successful business man who researched and chose to go to Mexico and have a gastric sleeve surgery. He'd actually taken 15 of his loved ones to the same clinic, and they all had the same surgery with the same inspiring results. His story softened my husband's heart in a miraculous way. Tony came home and told me what he felt God had just done and that he was going to trust God and send me for the surgery. I immediately fell to my destroyed knees and sobbed like a baby with gratitude and praise. Before I had gone to heaven, my husband hardly believed in God. Now he was trusting God at a level I would have never thought possible. I was frantic to make the arrangements before this miracle wore off. Within six weeks I had my surgery, and within six months I had lost 100 pounds.

It was a great day when I surprised my surgeon. I had to show him a picture, so he remembered me. I explained how his hard words were the warning from God I needed and thanked him for them. I insisted we replace both knees at once; he again said that's considered inhumane pain. I insisted. I refused to waste more time not doing what God put me here to do. I presented him with a note from my doctor stating I could handle the pain and would work hard at rehabilitation. Reluctantly, he agreed, and I had both knees replaced at the same time. My healing was speedy and miraculous.

My rehabilitation was to last four to six months, but after two months my physical therapists were convinced that I was done, but I was not. The morning of my surgery I told my surgeon I had been on my knees praying over him and his team. My surgeon smirked and jokingly said, "Well that's the last time you'll do that; I hope it was a good one." I was stunned when I heard that. The thought of not praying on my knees went through my soul like a sword. I insisted on praying on my knees since heaven. It put me right back at Jesus' feet in beautiful intimate flashbacks.

I was immediately hit with the reverent holiness of His sacrifice. I see the huge hole in His feet, and I'm transported right back to His perfect love for me. I would prefer to have my legs cut off at the knee than never be able to kneel again to pray. I caught my breath and reassured myself the surgeon's warning was not God's word. I explained again to my surgeon that I'd been to heaven, and God was about to change his opinion of what was possible. Now at my two-month physical therapy appointment, the therapists were convinced I was ready to graduate. I politely refused. I had my surgical follow up appointment the next morning, and I wasn't leaving therapy until I had learned how to successfully get on my knees to praise God for this miracle. My therapists both thought I was joking but soon realized I was serious and unwilling to listen to any explanation or warning of why this was a bad idea. They had a meeting and finally caved into my demands. I joyfully winced as they navigated getting me to my knees. But I did it. Two months after a bilateral knee replacement, I was finally back on my knees. I was ecstatic that God allowed me this merciful blessing. I insisted my therapists realize the significance of what they had just seen. I asked them to pray with me on my knees to help me celebrate this miracle, and they obliged me.

The next day I couldn't wait to see the look on my surgeon's face when he read the reports of my miraculous progress. He wasn't nearly as joyful as I was. He saw my miracle as an insane act of stubbornness until I went through my list of what God had done in my life since he had first met me over a year prior. First, he had warned me I'd never lose the weight, but I did. Second, he warned me I'd never get my knees replaced, especially at the same time, but I did. Lastly, he warned me it was impossible to get on my knees after replacement, but I did only eight weeks after. A year later my doctor said he'd like to put me on a billboard on the interstate, advertising his company's success in my life.

Shortly after my knee replacements I bought a beautiful red sports bike. My motorcycle was another symbol of God's miracle in my healing as it tells the world, I can do all things through Christ who gives me strength.

WHO AM I?

It seems all the rage to label people correctly as to not offend them. I find this silly and divisive. If the ultimate goal is to remember we're all human, beautifully and wonderfully made, why must we get so hell-bent on labeling everything.

Many years after my time in heaven I attended a women's retreat. I was going with a friend's church, excited for fellowship. Upon arrival, I had to fill out the registration card, "No problem, this should only take a second, then we can hit the buffet," I thought. I spent a minute and filled out my form, but the last question left me puzzled. It asked my faith. That seemed easy enough, I proudly wrote "Christian" and handed my form to the registration lady. She quickly scanned my card and abruptly whispered to the other registration lady, "What do I do about this?" I curiously laughed and asked if there was a problem. The ladies responded, "Your answer was too vague. You need to be more specific." They handed back my card, and I erased "Christian" and wrote, "Born Again Christian." They looked at my response and went back to whispering. Meanwhile, I was holding up a line of tired and hungry women and the registration ladies were getting frustrated. "Mam, we need to know your faith. It's a very simple question. You're making it very difficult to place you in a cabin. This is a Baptist retreat, so we need to know what type of Baptist you are." I scratched my head and thought, "I think she's serious, but I feel like I'm in a Saturday Night Live sketch right now." I explained that I'm actually not "Baptist," and they both were exasperated. I explained I'd been raised Baptist however, and that seemed to calm them a wee bit. They insisted on knowing which type of Baptist I was as a youth. I only irritated them further when I asked if I was being punked. They weren't going to let me register unless I chose a specific brand of Baptist from off their list, which seemed as lengthy as the Cheesecake Factory menu. I explained that I was shown in heaven by Jesus how it hurts him deeply to see His children dividing themselves within the body of Christ, focusing on our differences rather than what connects us. I pleaded my best case, that God is love, and love is to be multiplied not divided. My pleas obviously fell on deaf ears, so I closed my eyes and pointed to a faith label on the menu, and they let me in. I couldn't get mad although I was certainly frustrated. Before heaven, I was such a Pharisee. I knew the rules and loved to get righteously angry when others weren't obeying God's laws. I really believed my judgement and condemnation of others made me more discerning. Yet God gently humbled me when I was an arrogant self-righteous, Pharisee. I'm so grateful for His mercy. I would have beat me down hard if I were God. I couldn't be mad. I could only thank God for delivering me from the bondage of my former self. Many of my best lessons are Log and Speck scenarios. It's when I find a disturbing flaw in someone else that I realize God is showing me the same flaw in myself.

You hypocrite, first take the plank out of your own eye, and then you will see clearly to remove the speck out of your brother's eye. Matthew 7:5 NIV

I love that the plank and speck are both parts of the same thing. I am sometimes irritated by qualities in others. People who think they're so funny drive me crazy, but I try not to let it get to me. I'm Whende 2.0, the Heaven Edition. Now I try to laugh when I feel a judgy thought coming on and tell the Lord, "Well played Father. Message received loud and clear." I repent and repeat. Particularly with fellow believers who are more focused on rules than love, it's a constant struggle for me, seeing the body of Christ divided by its labels. We need to tear down the barriers between us and celebrate our King and His grace.

In the Bible we're referred to as sheep. Shortly after I began my intensive Bible study of Isaiah, our leader spoke to us about the nature of sheep. She taught us how stupid sheep are. They often freeze to death because they don't have the sense to come out from the cold. She told of an incident in Turkey. As shepherds ate their breakfast, a sheep wandered off and walked off the edge of a cliff, falling 15 meters to its death. The other 1,499 sheep followed. Four hundred sheep died in this tragedy. The others landed in a soft woolly pile. They say it cost the local sheep farmers over $76,000, all because the shepherds sat down on the job. Sheep are dumb defenseless followers. They're prone to wander even when all their needs are being met. A sheep can have beautiful pastures, clean water to drink, and they will still wander off. I think we humans are prone to do the same. If the shepherd isn't careful, he can easily loose his sheep. Thankfully, our shepherd never grows weary. Sheep are also completely defenseless against predators. They depend on their shepherd for complete protections. Their shepherd must always stay alert to protect them from their own stupidity.

Having been to heaven, I told myself, "I'm no longer a stupid sheep. I've been to heaven. I'm enlightened." On my way to Bible Study one morning I was talking to God and thanking him that I was no longer a stupid sheep like I used to be. I was planning on delicately explaining this to my group during discussion. I prayed for God to guide my words, so I wouldn't hurt the sweet sheep in my group's feelings. I was praising God for my sheep-to-shepherd transformation when it occurred to me, I'm prone to being foolishly arrogant. I reluctantly decided to ask God to give me a sign if I'm really still a stupid sheep in constant need of His shepherding. The moment I asked, I rounded a corner in my car, and directly in front of my car were three huge sheep charging directly toward me. I almost crashed trying to avoid hitting them.

These were the biggest sheep I'd ever seen, and God was making sure I saw these huge stupid sheep charging headlong into traffic. It was as if he were saying, "Honey, you're not just a dumb sheep, you're the biggest."

If I were to choose a label for myself before heaven, it would have been Woman of God, or Supermom. My label after the refiner's fire is "sheep." We're all God's sheep. The moment we think we're more, we become arrogant and judgmental, and our eternal rewards vanish from our Garments of Glory.

LIFE IS THE TEST

I met a precious lady in my Bible study in 2015 about the same time I started being asked to speak at churches. I loved her, and she prayed over me, and I can't tell you what that meant to me after losing my mom a few years prior. She came to hear me speak at my first speaking gig. I was a wreck but drew great strength knowing she was praying me up. After this event, we went out to eat, and she was tearful. She was very touched by my story and asked if I'd join her writing class at a local church. This class was called "Write Your Life." I couldn't accept her invitation fast enough, and so I met this powerful group of writers who were highly educated, and a few were even published authors. The catch was that I had to have something written for each week's class. I had so many ministries that I wasn't giving enough energy to, where would I find time to write? I was also now a grandmother which was my favorite calling ever. How would I devote myself to be a good writer and be good at all my other obligations? I decided to let God worry about those details. So, I joined this intimidating group of godly writers. I grew to love them and their precious stories. It was as if listening to each one of them weekly affected different aspects of my writing. It quickly became apparent God orchestrated this group beautifully. We prayed, laughed, and cried together. We were a family connected by the need to write down our stories for our children and future generations. Our stories all shared a core value that God's hand was in every detail of our lives

I couldn't help but cherish my new mentor who I started affectionately calling "Momma." I grew to love and respect this woman beyond words. She couldn't drive, which caused her sadness, but it was a blessing for me. She and I were able to spend much time together as I became her driver. I gave her laughter as she mentored and prayed for me daily. She helped me learn to say no and held me accountable.

As iron sharpens iron, so one person sharpens another. Proverbs 27:17 NIV

Momma felt my story was imperative in helping others, and she believed in me. I was told again to stop all my ministries and tell my story. Not serving God is harder for me than not eating, and I'm a fat kid. Mamma held my feet to the fire lovingly and reminded me my ministries wouldn't die without me. God would make a way. She wisely reminded me that the sooner I finished my book, the sooner I could go back to serving.

I've been very careful in telling my story to focus on my Father Jesus, His love, and how it affected my life after my death. What matters is my story could so easily be your story. So many people have heard me speak and confided they knew my story was true because the exact same thing had happened to them. I don't understand why they're not shouting from the mountaintops trying desperately to save everyone they love for Jesus, but through the years God has shown me that my gift is telling my story and not to question their journey.

Perhaps God chose me because I'm a big mouth. I've often thought (since getting kicked out of heaven) that my only spiritual gift was volume. I am also flexible as I often put my foot in my mouth. I wasn't given an inside voice by my heavenly Father. I've always been ashamed of how loud I am, but perhaps my childlike enthusiasm and ADHD are His brilliant design to help me get people fired up for the awesomeness of heaven. I now know that the things I've always disliked about myself have made me exactly who God created me to be. I'm a Christian speaker who doesn't need a microphone.

I've grown to love sharing my story with strangers everywhere I go. The cashiers at my favorite stores all call me the Heaven Lady. I'm unscathed by people who don't believe my story. I might not have believed it had it not happened to me.

The devil has thrown incredible hurdles at me, even trying to kill me. I'm still here against all odds. When I say the devil tried to kill me, I mean if it weren't for God's hand on me, I surely would have died. Almost immediately after filming the first talk show, my new friend warned me that the devil would try to kill me very soon because he didn't want me to write this book, but I just laughed the warning off.

Four days later, Tony and I were vacationing in Santa Cruz, California. I was sleeping in my 5-star hotel early in the morning when a painful zap in my left arm woke me up. I flicked off the creature that had hurt me and was surprised to hear it hit the wall across the room. I had vaguely seen a clear/golden insect about an inch and a half long before I launched him. It stung, but my pain tolerance is higher than average, so I chose to ignore it. Within two weeks, I had black swollen veins in that area and throbbing pain. My fingers were numb, and I wasn't sleeping because of the pain. I finally agreed to go to the Urgent Care. The doctor assessed the wound and decided it wasn't a bite, as I had thought, but a sting. She intently studied the bite/sting charts and became very alarmed. She told me I had been stung by a very deadly scorpion and told me it was too late for some anti-venom, and I had a serious case of sepsis. She put me on an intense cycle of antibiotics. I assured the doctor I would be fine, but I was hurting everywhere. I continued working and teaching Sunday school, but I couldn't hardly form a sentence. The sepsis seemed stronger than I was on most days. I slowly started to recover; however, within two months I had double pneumonia, incredible shoulder pain, and no feeling in my blackening arm and hand. My husband drug me into the ER. I don't like being in hospitals, and since heaven I hate being pitied. Within an hour of testing, I was told I had had a huge blockage/clot between my left shoulder and my heart. It had managed to dislodge on its own which meant it was going to be in my lungs. I wouldn't be leaving the hospital for quite some time – if ever. The doctors and nurses were upset that I didn't seem concerned. I casually explained that I was fine, and I knew the devil was just trying to interfere with my mission and scare me. I continued trying to assure the hospital staff I would be leaving soon, but they insisted I call my immediate family and say goodbye. They convinced my husband and daughter that a pulmonary embolism this size was fatal, and I wasn't grasping the severity of my condition. I explained that the doctors didn't understand the sovereignty of my God. After several tests, I was told it was unexplainable that the clot was gone. No traces of it anywhere. I tried to get the doctors to admit they had just witnessed a miracle, but I couldn't. I left the hospital after more intense antibiotics and spent the next eight weeks leashed to an oxygen machine at home, and I recovered.

Fast forward a year, I was sitting on Timmy's talk show again sharing my story and basking in God's goodness. I didn't share the story of the scorpion because I saw God's hand in my life daily. It really wasn't a big deal. My dear friend Tim was interviewing me on the changes in my life since my first appearance on his show. He, after all, had had a huge part in me writing this book. I excitedly explained how I knew the devil was scared of me. He'd like to end my life, but I wasn't scared because I knew my God would protect me.

Almost immediately after filming ended, two random friends both called me with urgent warnings. They each separately gave me the same message. They told me they knew that God wanted them to warn me that the devil wanted me dead the week before my book was finished. The second friend told me God would send an angel to save me, and my angel would get pretty beat up, but I would be ok. However, this attack of the devil would be worse than the first.

Just a few days later, I was at Evergreen Speedway in Monroe, Washington for the 2017 Rory Price Memorial Race. I was watching my husband race our Sprint car in the main event. He was doing well about 10 laps in when a Sprint car directly in front of him lost control, flying off the track at full speed (well over 100 mph) at Turn 3. I heard the motor winding tight as it became airborne. Before I knew it, I was hit by that car, crushed between my golf cart and a chain link safety fence. The car had rammed a giant safety barrier into the fence pinning me. I was dazed by the impact, and I couldn't see my legs from the knees down and immediately went into shock. I remember thinking, "Wow I just lost my legs, but I didn't die; I win devil," as I slipped into unconsciousness. When I regained consciousness, I was being cradled by a track official. Maybe I was in shock, but I was happy that I survived another awesome injury, this time in front of thousands of witnesses. I assured the numerous medics that night at the track in the ambulance and at the hospital that Jesus saved me. He wasn't through with me yet. I assumed my legs were crushed at the very least. They appeared to be very lumpy and significantly cut up. I was so excited that finally a huge audience was witness to the incredible miracles God performed in my life. No one could say my surviving this crash with lack of injury wasn't a miracle. The grandstands were full of people who assumed I was dead. Even though I knew my legs may be amputated, I celebrated and praised God for giving me more time to finish my book and share my story. It was an opportunity to earn some big eternal rewards like my heroes: Corrie Ten Boom, Joni Eareckson, or Mother Theresa. I shared my story with many first responders. I'd ask them, "Do you know Jesus?" They'd respond, "Do you know what day it is? Who is the President?" I'd tell them (while I am slipping in out of consciousness), "Don't talk to me about politics. I'm trying to save you from eternal fire and torture." Evidently, my first responders weren't supposed to discuss their beliefs with clients. "Ok guys, but I'm the customer today, and the customers always right. So, listen. I'm going to be great with or without legs. God is going to bless me. He has kicked me out of heaven. I have a mission; I need to know that before I get out of this ambulance you all will share my story with people you're trying to save as they're drawing their last breath. Heaven is real, and Jesus Christ is the only way to get there. You must tell them to repent from their sins. Heaven is better than anything you can imagine. It's like you've finally woken up from your worst nightmare the second you arrive." The medics were listening. I made an impression. I told everyone listening about my miracle. I couldn't contain my excitement that I had proof. In the X-ray room, they took several images of my seemingly shattered lower legs, so if I did need them removed or became scarred with surgeries, I would have proof for my testimony. I praised God for my angel that surely took the brutal worst of my injury.

Three hours later after tons of x-rays and exams, I left the hospital with no broken bones or stitches. I was hit by a flying race car doing well over 100 miles per hour, and I was fine. I had yet another validation of my story and God's hand upon me.

FAITH VERSUS FEAR

Eighteen years after my time in heaven, God sent me a prophet. He revealed my purpose of being sent back. He told me millions would hear my story and forever be changed. I had felt like a disgruntled Israelite wandering the desert for 40 years until I received that revelation. But I was again frustrated. How could this man know God's plan for me and clearly hear God's voice, but I could not? I'd been at the feet of Jesus in heaven, but when I begged to hear God speak to me, all I heard was a big fat chasm of silence.

God sent me several prophets. All strangers I'd never met, all telling me the same thing in different words. It was becoming clear this wasn't hocus pocus mumbo jumbo as I'd always thought. God was communicating to me through strangers who'd never been to heaven. I started purposefully asking and seeking answers as to why God chose them and not me to share His voice with. He was giving them such a gift. I was jealous and frustrated that this gifting was not in me.

Prophets were still a thing. How could I have gone to heaven and not known this? I saw firsthand in heaven all Jesus' life and miracles, many not even recorded in the Bible. I knew firsthand the power of the Holy Spirit. I knew Jesus was completely human and only able to perform miracles because of the power of the Holy Spirit. Could it be that these prophets sent to me by the Lord had more Holy Spirit than I had? I'd been to heaven. They hadn't. The Bible says our giftings are as great as our faith, so why didn't I have the gifts of the Holy Spirit?

I know my mother always prayed for the gift of speaking in tongues, but to be honest, if I'd had seen her do it, I'd probably have freaked out. I wasn't even sure what all the gifts of the Holy Spirit were, but I wanted everything Jesus promised His disciples. Before Jesus went back to heaven, He told His disciples He was giving them the gift of the Holy Spirit so that they could perform miracles and continue His work, doing even greater things than Jesus.

I tell you the truth, anyone who believes in me will do the same works I have done, and even greater works, because I am going to be with the Father. You can ask for anything in my name, and I will do it, so that the Son can bring glory to the Father. Yes, ask me for anything in my name, and I will do it. John 14:12-14 NLT

That was over 2,000 years ago. The Bible clearly states that the same power that rose Jesus from the dead lives in us. I always assumed the "us" meant "them." I certainly had never raised anyone from the dead. I had never given anyone a message from God. I had never healed the sick nor cured the lame nor given vision to the blind. I've been to heaven, so if I couldn't do those things after being in the presence of Jesus for what felt like three lifetimes, how could the disciples?

The answer to these questions began when I was reunited with my best friend Jennifer from high school who saved my life and gave me a home when I was a prodigal teenager. This happened shortly after I received my first prophetic message. It was awesome to see her again, but I was nervous and very apprehensive to get in a close friendship because our lives through high school were during a time I had been so ashamed of and had been trying to put behind me for years. I wasn't that person anymore. I wanted to put that period of rebellion and sin behind me and never look back. But I felt I owed her so much. After all, without her I surely would have killed myself. She rescued me, taking this prodigal daughter off the streets and gave me a home. Jen was a Christian and had a relationship with God. We didn't often speak about it back then because we were both too cool, but we knew each other's truth. We simply chose sin back then and drew our strength from each other not the Lord.

Jen now owned a salon and started cutting my hair. It was like no time had passed. Catching up with Jennifer was like going home again. She told me she was completely sold out for Jesus now, and she seemed completely different than the Jennifer I once knew, still strong and stable but now humbler and more self-aware. I explained that I too was sold out to Jesus, but only because He had given me a reality check I couldn't refuse. He had taken me to heaven against my will and shown me my life in live action 4D, and then Jesus' life of sacrifice. I was certain Jen would think I'd lost my mind. I was concerned that I wasn't spiritually mature enough to restart a friendship with Jennifer again. We reminisced about great memories, and it was awesome. Jen and I shared what God had done in our lives. I could tell she was on the fence deciding if I was crazy or not. She knew the old me possibly better than anyone on earth, but she kept asking questions as if trying to trip me up biblically. I'd answer and ask her questions. I knew for her to see I'd truly changed, it would take more than one haircut, so I booked another appointment and hugged her tight and left. I was grateful for the opportunity to again thank her for what she'd done for me in a pivotal season of my youth. I hadn't realized that my heart had missed her so much. I left perplexed by how she had such faith and trust in God without having had a heaven experience. Jen wasn't the same at all. She even seemed more spiritually gifted than me, and she was hearing God's voice.

During our next haircut, I was full of questions, and so was she. I shared my encounter with the prophet who spoke to me from God and how he told me things only God could know. I thought it would blow her mind, but she explained this happened frequently in her circles. My mind was blown. I thought surely she was into some kind of sketchy psychic stuff. Jen invited me to an event at a local church, not a church I was familiar with, but a hippy, dippy, crazy church. She claimed these people could do amazing things and even hear the voice of God. I was skeptical, but there's nothing I wouldn't do to grow closer to God. If there's the slightest chance these folks had a spiritual gifting I didn't have, I needed to know why.

I felt the Father pushing me, so reluctantly I went. Jen was very excited as she met me at the door, but I did not want to be there. We went into this old school campus turned church, but this night it was set up in stations. In the sanctuary/gymnasium was worship and prophetic art, and in the classroom, there were prophetic word stations. In another room, there was a prophetic dance station, and in another area, there was a prophetic healing station, and in yet another place a prayer station. I was so out of my element; I felt like I was in a strange foreign culture. I also felt like I stood out like a sore thumb because my skepticism was surely visible to these strange people who seemed suspiciously too happy. More than once since heaven I had been called a sunshine suppository. I had been to heaven, so it makes sense for me to radiate joy, but these folks were so loving and happy, it seemed concerning. I could immediately feel the Holy Spirit powerfully upon my arrival, and Jennifer was thrilled. How could she see these people and see God in them when I'd been to heaven? After five minutes of observing worship, I thought they all needed to be medicated. I felt the Holy Spirit so strongly, but I was literally having a battle between my mind and soul. I felt physically ill. It was bazaar because I've always been the brave one, not the chicken. My internal gauge for feeling the Holy Spirit (I'd developed since heaven) worked accurately, and it was telling me to stay. I persevered although I wanted to run away and escape this craziness. Jen was happily signing us up for the stations while I immediately found the snack table and started self-comforting with carbs to cope.

We went to the first station, a large room where there were chairs set up in fours, one in the middle and three facing around it. I was asked to sit in the center chair, and the three strangers greeted me warmly and introduced themselves. They explained that they would like to pray over me and ask God if He had a message for me. My fight or flight instinct was now fully engaged. I believed people could certainly hear God's will, but there were five or six groups of four in this room. How could this many people hear God's voice, and I who'd been to heaven couldn't? My Holy Spirit gauge was on fire, burning in my chest like Iron Man's light. I tried to appear calm and used my Lamaze breathing technique and stayed. I kept praying in my spirit that if God was growing me and this was His will, that He'd make it obvious. The three strangers prayed over me quietly with such love. After a quiet pause, the first fellow (who looked remarkably sane and normal) told me God showed him that I was a happy, yellow, heart shaped leaf blowing through the air and enjoying the sunshine as it danced through life wherever the wind blew it, but not wanting to land until it found the water. It felt like it belonged in the water. The second person smiled and said God showed her the same thing. A beautiful golden leaf dancing in the wind. The third lady smiled gently and squeezed my hand and said that for me, the water represents heaven, and I was aching to get there, but the wind represents God's will. She said I'm a yellow leaf because yellow represents joy, and I joyfully go wherever God sends me. The dancing in the wind represents life's twists and turns, but I'm joyful and willing to go wherever I'm sent without hesitation. They asked me if their words made sense, and I sat there dumbfounded. I couldn't wrap my brain around how accurately simplified their vision of my life was. They told me God delighted in me in a way they'd never seen. I must have a tremendous anointing or calling on my life, and then they asked me to pray over them. They each wanted me to put my hands on them and pray over them. But when I did, they each slightly jumped. They said it felt as though they got a warm shock. This was so weird, but I indulged them and prayed over each of them.

The next station was a prophetic art center. I uncomfortably sat at a table, and a kind lady asked me if she could pray over me. I welcomed her to, and as she reached over the table to put her hand on mine, she slightly jumped upon making contact. She smiled sheepishly and apologized. She said that had never happened to her before, but she grabbed my arm tighter and said she got a warm tickly shock upon touching me. (At this point I started looking for a walkie talkie or earpiece. How did she know that was the other people's response?) She prayed as I sat skeptically watching her go to work drawing with chalks a tiny island in a big light blue ocean with a single palm tree bending before a beautiful sun. The palm tree was bending so much that its fronds were touching the water. She explained that heaven was the ocean, and I was the tree whose fronds or leaves were straining toward the ocean desperately longing to be in the water. The big beautiful sun was The Holy Spirit, and I so deeply enjoyed His warmth. She asked if I had any questions about what she had just drawn for me, and if it made sense. I just sat there puzzled, trying to understand why her message so similarly reflected the message I had just received an in an entirely different building by an entirely different group of people.

Jen's prophetic art and word was as uniquely similar to her life and events as mine were, which was amazing. We sat down and discussed how mind-blowing this was, but I still remained stoically cynical and skeptical. There was no logical explanation for these peoples' giftings when they hadn't been to heaven, and I had. I felt it was absolutely impossible for them to love the Lord more than I did, and yet they had gifts I didn't.

Then, we prepared for the speaker as the worship began. Immediately, people were on their feet dancing with their hands stretched to the heavens in a level of worship I had never experienced on earth. These people were dancing with silk flags like hippies at Woodstock, with no care of who was watching, dancing like it was just them and Jesus. Some were on their knees with arms stretched out to heaven, tears streaming down their faces as if they were pleading for their lives. As I observed, my Holy Spirit gauge was reaching new levels, but my brain was doubting and uncomfortable with all that was going on around me. I was baffled; how can my Holy Spirit meter be telling me one thing and my brain telling me another? Was I so trapped in my religious upbringing that I was unable to absorb the Holy Spirit working around me? I'm the lady who speaks on a stage telling people to bust down their walls of religion and that God is preparing us for new things. Surely, I could not be one of those "religious" people that I preach to. Everybody around me was deeply absorbed in praising and worshipping, and here I was having an inner argument with the Lord, asking him, "Father, if this is legit and real, and not some form of a cult or sorcery, give me a sign if it's me who needs to grow deeper."

Soon after, the speaker finished his powerful message, and I realized I was grateful I had come. Then he said, "Ok, it's time to have some fun. We're about to break off some religious spirits in this house of the Lord today." I was excited because I love doing that as a speaker – until what he said next. He asked for all of the audience to come to the front of the auditorium where the people on his staff and the church staff formed two lines facing each other. He called this a "fire tunnel" and explained that we were going to walk through the channel of leaders, and the people on either side of this human tunnel would put their hands in the air praying over us as we walk through single file. They would bless us and prayerfully stir up the Holy Spirit in us. This sounded like lunacy to me, but Jen encouraged me to participate. Only because I was so deeply indebted to her, did I obliged.

Trepidatious didn't begin to describe my feelings. The term "fire tunnel" sounded like a horror novel. I got in the long winding line and wondered what these people were seeking so desperately. They were jonesing for Jesus like addicts for drugs. This had to be a cult. I watched shaking my head as people slowly made their way through the prayer channel. Some were laughing, some crying, some even crawling as they laughed and cried their way through. The most disturbing, however, were the ones who seemed drunk. These wack-a-doodles were out of control. Jen seemed delighted by the power she felt God was outpouring on these masses. I stoically observed and prayed. I asked God to please explain why my Holy Spirit sonar was clearly now defective. It had worked seemingly perfect until now. My soul wanted the Holy Spirit, and my feet wanted to run like Forrest Gump. I felt like I'd been trying to do long division in my head all evening and constantly getting the wrong answer with no way to find the right one. When I got to the tunnel, people seemed to be getting lightly shocked when they put their praying hands on me, but I'd just decided to deal with it. However, when I got to the middle of the tunnel, I came to the speaker who had just delivered his powerful message, and he put his hands on me to pray. We were both amazed when he was shocked so hard that he fell back on the stage steps. I was mortified, but the crazy train I was in didn't even seem to notice. I started walking harder trying to gently push the people through, so I could escape. We finally exited the tunnel and headed to leave. I don't know when it happened, but Jen's train had jumped the tracks. She shared as we walked to our cars how amazing the evening was and how stirred up she was in the Spirit. I agreed. I was certainly stirred up in the Spirit, but I was from different viewpoint than my formerly brilliant and discerning friend. We hugged goodbye, and I spoke to God in my car the entire hour drive home. What just happened? Was it witchcraft or sorcery? How could my soul be so happy but my mind so distraught? How would I tell Jen this was not of the Lord when I felt His presence so strongly? How could Jen be so wise and yet so gullible?

At my next haircut, we reflected on our evening, and I had prayerfully asked God to help me lovingly ask Jen questions that would help her see the truth rather than blatantly telling her my opinion and sounding disrespectful. As I sat in her chair, the Holy Spirit began to stir up in me. We discussed how accurate our prophetic words had been. The more we discussed, the warmer I became. Not uncomfortably like a hot flash, but like a tingly peaceful comfort starting in my upper gut and then through my extremities. My hands were on fire just from discussing what God had done. The more I spoke of it the warmer my body became. I could feel my faith actually growing.

Jen believed it all, but I was still trying to cautiously discern.

At this point, I had shared my heaven story at a few churches and women's retreats locally. I had developed or become a part of many powerful ministries. My reputation as a woman of God and integrity was everything to me. I couldn't be affiliated with anything that could be perceived as untrue or, God forbid, a cult.

Upon leaving Jen's salon that day, the Holy Spirit's burning in me was so strong I had to let it out before I exploded. I stopped at the store for groceries. I had to use a mobility scooter because my knee pain was out of control. I robotically drove through the warehouse store, filling my cart and pondering my conversation with Jen and the burning in my spirit. I was getting out of my mobility scooter to unload my groceries when a tender-hearted store employee asked if he could help me unload my groceries into my car. I typically detest help of any kind, but I felt such a warm loving burning in my spirit that I thought maybe God brought this guy to me. So, I internally prayed as he helped me unload. I insisted he be careful not to strain his back lifting my heavy boxes, and he shared he already had a back injury. I shared my heaven story with him as I typically do with anyone I meet for more than 30 seconds. I explained how powerful the absence of pain was in heaven. Because of what I'd experienced at that supernatural event, I felt motivated to pray for him to be healed. I asked him to let me pray over his back pain before he returned my scooter. I couldn't wait to get my hands on him. They were very hot, and I was so stirred up in the Holy Spirit. Even though I wasn't used to this feeling, I hoped God would heal him. As I was praying for healing and blessings on his home, his health, his finances, and his future, I felt a warm wave of overwhelming love come over me. I asked God to gently draw him into deeper intimacy, allowing him to see himself through the eyes of Jesus, so he would know how pursued he was by pure love. I thanked God for blessing me by allowing me to meet this precious man and pray over him in Jesus name. My hands were still on fire as I ended my prayer.

I opened my eyes and there was such joy and relief in his eyes. I was unaware he'd been crying. He said his whole body was hot and tingly since the moment I touched him. He knew he was healed, and he was so grateful. He then explained that this morning he had planned to kill himself when he got home from work that evening. He couldn't bare his constant pain which made him feel unloved by God. He had everything, including his goodbye notes to family, ready at home waiting after he got off work. That morning, he told God, "Today's your last chance; if you're real, and you love me, prove it, or tonight I die." I sobbed joyfully as I heard his story. As I wept over him in Costco's parking lot, I told him of the overwhelming love I felt for him from the heavenly Father. I just wanted to rock him and hold him like a baby and cover him with kisses.

As I left the store that day with tears rolling down my face praising and worshiping my Father, I felt a convicted in my heart. I am so prideful in general. Helping people is my greatest joy. However, I am far too prideful to ever let anyone help me. Even though I couldn't walk, I would typically refuse a mobility cart because someone far more deserving may need it like a Veteran or senior citizen. I hated being needy. It was so out of character for me to allow that man to help me unload my groceries into my car. If I hadn't listened to the stirring in my spirit and humbled myself by allowing him to help me, it would have had a horrible outcome. Instead, I left that man praising God for his new reason to live – his joy and health restored.

I share my heaven story with almost everyone I meet. I don't care if they believe me or think I'm crazy. Life on earth is short. In a blink of an eye we'll be at the feet of Jesus, and I might show up in their life's highlight reel.

HOLY SPIRIT ACADEMY

Jen soon discovered a Holy Spirit school that taught how to develop the giftings of the Holy Spirit, a ministry school here in Salem, Oregon at the same church that gave me several accurate prophecies. She was excited and insisted we both attend together. She said her spiritual mentor encouraged us as it was the natural next step in our journey of faith. Jen begged me to go, but I was adamant this school couldn't teach me anything I didn't already learn in heaven. I prayed and decided to indulge Jen because I had to protect her if this was a trap of the devil.

I called the school to register for the orientation class but explained I would not be enrolling. I politely explained I'd been to heaven and didn't need this schooling. Furthermore, I didn't believe in their portrayal of faith. I was simply indulging a friend whom I owed so much to.

Upon arriving at the school, I prayed earnestly in my car. "Lord I don't want to be a chicken if you're calling me deeper, but I don't believe in a school claiming to develop the gifts of the Holy Spirit. Either I've been gifted with them or I haven't. So, I need to see a bigtime sign from You, if You want me to go to the school."

I had met three clearly anointed people in my life at this point. They all told me the same things:

1. I was covered in gold dust, sparkly and shiny like they'd never seen before and almost glowing.

2. I had enviable freedom and joy.
3. God delighted in me powerfully.

I asked God if He wanted me to attend this crazy school that was so out of my comfort zone, to send me a true prophet with any of those words and stir my Holy Spirit sonar, so I would be certain this was not a trick of the enemy.

I went in, shields engaged, so no hocus pocus mumbo jumbo would fool me. I was a warrior of discernment. I got in the line for the buffet when a man, who looked much like the colored pencils angel who changed my life, came alongside me and warmly greeted me. He stared at me and said there was something very special about me that I was glowing like I was golden. Then smiled even bigger and said, "God delights so powerfully in you; you have a beautiful and enviable freedom in Christ."

Within my first 30 seconds of arriving, God had exceeded my request. I asked for one of the things I'd previously been told by true prophets, and God gave me three. My Spirit was also on fire. This kind man sat down to eat with me, and I knew I was being told by God I would have to attend. My spirit was happy and on fire like it was at the feet of Jesus, but my brain was not.

I listened as the teachers explained how Jesus left us with a tremendous gift, the Holy Spirit. Jesus told us we were to act on His behalf using the gifts of the Holy Spirit to do His work. This gift had no expiration date, and it would help us heal the sick and even raise the dead. The same power that rose Jesus from the dead lives in every follower of Jesus. I had experienced this intense power in heaven; it was like lightening coursing through my body. I knew every word in the Bible was true, but I felt far from powerful. I struggled keeping my plants alive. Raising the dead definitely wasn't on my resume.

The teacher asked us where in the Bible was the expiration date for these gifts? Hummm… good question. He then explained the baptism of the Holy Spirit. I'd already been water baptized, so I thought I had this in spades. It turns out this was something different. Just as John the Baptist said:

"I baptize you with water for repentance. But after me comes one who is more powerful than I, whose sandals I am not worthy to carry. He will baptize you with the Holy Spirit and fire." NIV

The baptism of repentance was what I had experienced. This other baptism was a new concept and seemed very strange. How exactly is one baptized in the Holy Spirit? The teacher then told of people getting the gifts of speaking in tongues upon Holy Spirit baptism, and they often had encounters with God after being baptized this way. I was doubtful. I'd been to heaven; I surely was full of the Holy Spirit. I watched as this teacher played videos from Bethel Church in California where crazy miracles happen often. The teachings we were to learn in this class were coming directly from Bethel. I decided I needed to go to the source and investigate. Everything the teacher in the video presented made sense, and most importantly, he backed it up scripturally, but I needed to see the source for myself before I wasted any more time in class. I needed to know this was of God and nothing else.

To investigate, I went on a six-hour road trip to Bethel Church in Redding, California with my friend Jen and her four-year-old daughter. We arrived Friday evening in time for worship. I was impressed upon arrival at how legit this place looked. It was beautiful and big. My Holy Spirit sonar was glowing. We entered the sanctuary and I was amazed. It wasn't in any way scary as I'd expected. I could tangibly feel the presence of God more than any other earthly place I'd been. We enjoyed the worship and the wisdom of the speaker. After the service, a young woman who'd been sitting behind me asked if she could give me a message from God. I was excited to hear what this girl had to say. She told me God was turning a new page in my book, that I would be stretched in new ways, but my story wasn't over. I needed to trust Him and my discernment. She told me He delights in me in a powerful way like she'd never seen. She described a heat in her upper abdomen as an intense joy that she hadn't felt before. She smiled as I explained to her that's where my Holy Spirit gauge was. I shared my story with her. She was a student at the school at Bethel that I was attending via video. It was amazing, that this girl, still a teenager, was so gifted. She'd never been to heaven but clearly heard the voice of God. She was shy but bold enough to say things that must have seemed crazy to her. I wanted the giftings this girl was working with. She prayed over me and encouraged me to come to witness the healings the next day. She said it would be the perfect time to see God at work and be baptized in the Holy Spirit if I felt led to.

That night I slept well, grateful for my message from God, although I still felt stretched. The next morning I felt I'd have my answers and see for myself if this was smoke and mirrors, or God's wonders. I prayed earnestly that God would help me see His truth.

We arrived at Bethel and signed up for a healing. I now had my new knees, so I really had nothing left to heal, but I signed up to intercede for my husband's back. It was a spy mission really. I had to get into the healing room so I could see if this was legit. We were in a group of about 20 people, being ushered into a large classroom. Two teachers showed us scriptures about healings on a large screen. They then asked how many of us were there from out of state. Everyone raised their hands. They asked how many of us were from out of the country, and two thirds of the class raised their hands. I was astonished. How had these people heard of this healing place from all over the world? I lived only six hours away and had just learned of it. These people had gone to great lengths to be there. They were there (many with care providers) expecting a miracle.

After learning scriptural truths on how healing was used throughout God's Word, we were taken into a big room where many teams of three were healing the sick and broken. Upon entering, my soul was on fire. My brain wanted to flee, but my soul felt as if it were back in the presence of Jesus, walking through His life with him, mesmerized as he healed so many people. I resisted my urge to judge and prayed through my mounting discomfort as I took it all in.

There was a red velvet rope separating the healers from the sick. There were about 100 chairs for the sick to sit and wait for their turn. We took our seats as we watched what unfolded before us. People were laying on the floor smiling as if they were passed out drunk. Many were being prayed over by the prayer teams of three. The teams seemed very normal, concerned for the sick and trusting that God was at work. I was amazed at how they would go to a person in the waiting area, kindly greet them, read the paper we were required to have filled out, and walk them into an open spot on the floor. They would pray over them, and it seemed within a few moments these sick people would collapse into the floor. It bothered me that these people, many who could hardly stand, were falling into a heap, and the prayer team wasn't freaking out. I knew all too well how difficult it was to get off the floor with bad knees. These people were worse off than I had been, and I wondered why the prayer teams weren't concerned. They would simply get down on their knees and continue praying as the guest was passed out, then cover them with a small blanket and go get another guest. Although my Holy Spirit sonar was on fire, my brain was upset that they seemed without worry that these poor folks just collapsed. Furthermore, the prayer teams were completely convinced they were healed. I stared at this craziness for about 20 minutes, watching people wake up happily on the floor and get up healed. Many were shaky and had to be helped to a chair. I prayed that if this was legit, God would make it happen to me. But I had nothing to be healed of. I had new knees, and I had no physical or emotional pain. I just trusted God would tell me what to do and knew that He had me there for a reason. I started trying to see who I'd like to help me when my turn came. I saw a very gangsta-ish Mexican guy wearing a flat billed hat that said EX-ATHIEST. This thug was my kind of guy. He was evidently a turnaround story like me, so I prayed God would have his team pick me.

Within minutes of praying, the ex-atheist dude came up to me and asked if he could pray over me. His team seemed very cool; I was thrilled they chose me, but I was so nervous I was on fire.

They read my sheet and were confused that I had nothing written in the healing box. I quickly came clean and explained that I was there on a spy mission. I'd been to heaven, and I was writing a book about it. I wanted to go deeper to serve God better, and I needed to know if this was the true next step to hearing God's voice. They asked if I'd like to be baptized in the Holy Spirit, and I explained I was baptized in the name of the Father, Son, and Holy Spirit when I was eight years old, so that wasn't necessary. They said this was different, and I believed them. I thought, what do I have to lose? So, I explained that my spirit loved them, but my brain thought they were snake oil salesmen. I told them they were under no circumstances to touch me. I wasn't sure what drugs were on their hands, and I knew if this was real, they didn't need to touch me. My gangsta dude laughed as he signaled his team of other healers that I was finally here. I was confused. He explained that seven months ago God woke him up and told him he would soon baptize someone in the Holy Spirit who was even more stubborn than he was – someone writing a book. He would have the honor of changing her life, and she could finish her book to help countless others grow deeper in the Holy Spirit. Now I really had my shields up. All the team was excited, but I was triggered.

How could this be happening? I again explained that I was not like the others here, and I had no intention of collapsing or passing out. I was a cool cat. I was the Fonz. I again insisted nobody on the team touch me. My healing team couldn't help but giggle as two women moved behind me to catch me. Weren't they listening? It seemed the more I explained the less they believed me. I was frustrated and shut up, so we could get this over with, so I could prove them wrong. I agreed to let the dude baptize me in the Holy Spirit which seemed completely unnecessary since I'd been to heaven. But if I truly was the one this dude thought I was, I wanted it. He began to pray as I stood seeking God's will.

He thanked God for the honor of being a part of my story, and he thanked God for choosing Him to bless me and asked God to baptize me with the Holy... and before he could even say

Spirit, it felt as if every bone in my body suddenly dissolved. I collapsed. In a happily drunken slow-motion movie way, I felt back in heaven. My soul was at peace like it was in heaven, and I was pure energy again to at an extent I thought impossible on earth. I was disappointed in myself as I watched my prayer team try to cover me with a blanket. I objected and asked them to help me up, but they just walked away. I tried hard to get up and even called out to Jen and her daughter to come help me. I was too weak and shaky to get up. Why was everyone ignoring me? I decided to just lie back down and gather my strength. I was giggling as my whole body tingled. But I couldn't waste time. I needed to be watching Jen's daughter while Jen got her healing, but I could barely open my eyes, let alone sit up. Everyone seemed to ignore my requests for help as if I weren't there. Frustrated, finally I was able to sit up and be noticed. I had a blanket on me. When did this happen? I clearly remember telling the prayer team I didn't need one just seconds ago.

A team member helped me up and back to a seat next to Jen who was thrilled that I went down like a ton of bricks. I was weak and felt tipsy, and she asked me if I had a vision or what I felt when I passed out. What was she talking about? I did collapse but would certainly never pass out. She claimed I'd been passed out for 20 minutes. I told her I had been sitting up calling her and was upset she'd ignored my pleas for help. She laughed at me and said, "Dude you've been laying down for 20 minutes smiling like a drunk." I couldn't believe it. How was it I had gone down so easily? I'd intentionally locked my new knees, so I couldn't fall. Why did I feel so weak? And what did all these prayer teams stand to gain from this? They were all volunteers, unpaid.

I sat dazed as a team came and chose Jen, and she eagerly went super excited to be baptized in the Holy Spirit. The team prayed over her for healing first, and as soon as they asked God to baptize her in the Holy Spirit Jen went down. Not with the gazelle like grace I'm certain I fell with but like a tree in a hurricane. I watched as she joyfully basked in His presence for over an hour. When her team covered her with a blanket, her four-year-old daughter grew concerned. A team member came to Skylar to explain that her mommy was having some time with Jesus and not to worry but be happy for her mommy. Until then I was unaware why the people on the floor were so happy. I didn't know when we fainted, we were being given a gift of time with Jesus. I'd been trying so desperately to get up and remain cool that I had missed my gift. Again, my pride had blocked my blessing. I hugged Sky and we prayed mommy would have a great time with Jesus. Shortly after praying, Jen's belly started jumping up and down like I didn't think possible. She started laughing with tears streaming down her face as her tummy convulsed, completely unconscious. Half of me wanted to go shake her awake and tell her she looked like a nut. But I hardly had the strength to sit up, let alone stand. But I also was grateful she was getting a taste of what I experienced in heaven. She convulsed for over 20 minutes but was out for over an hour. Finally, Jen came to and was able to be helped up. She was drenched with sweat and tears. She was ecstatic and grateful for her encounter with God.

The healing service was ending, and we were asked if we'd like to give a testimony of our healing. Many people spoke of restored vision or hearing. One lady's deformed leg grew four inches, and she was out of her wheelchair walking. I was given the microphone and explained briefly that I'd been to heaven 22 years ago and was sure I'd been cut off from God, but today I felt him in a way I thought was impossible on earth. I thanked the teams for allowing God to heal me of pride and show me truth. I cried as I began to realize for 22 years I'd felt abandoned by my God because my pride kept me from going deeper. I didn't want to look like a lunatic flopping on the floor, speaking in tongues, etc. But if this was real, and it definitely was, I wanted more.

UNSEEN ADVENTURES

During the entire drive home from Bethel I remembered the pastor at my ministry school telling me he was once a cool cat too, but when he became baptized in the Holy Spirit, he started twitching like a tweaker for Jesus. I had assured him I was far cooler than he was, and I would never lose my composure. I just had my knees replaced, and I didn't get hurt when I fell, but I knew I drew the line at twitching like the pastor when the Holy Spirit came over me. Of course, I realize I'd told myself the same thing about collapsing. I was inwardly laughing at myself while also disgusted that I fought my collapse so hard that I missed my encounter with Jesus. I always thought these folks who were "slain in the spirit" were fakers/drama queens. But my experience was real, and I still felt weak. I had a lot to process and I typically process best through talking. I was excited to share my crazy encounter with my boys at home.

When I got home, I told my nephew Ben about all the awesome stuff I witnessed and felt at Bethel. It was obvious he thought I'd lost my fool mind. The Holy Spirit was still on me and I was visibly shaking. I was on fire excited that I was finally going deeper. I then told my son Austin, and this time as I got to the part of my story where I collapsed like a graceful gazelle, I started twitching hard. I could feel the Holy Spirit coming over me so strong. I thought, great Lord, because my heaven story doesn't make me sound crazy enough, and now I'm a tweaker? I scared my poor son. At this point I think it's safe to say my boys were ready to have me committed. I could feel my son's eyes sizing me up for a jacket that buckles in the back. I finally shut up and stopped trying to convince him it was the Holy Spirit, and that I wasn't crazy. We agreed to disagree.

The next week at class I was ready to dive deeper. I was committed to not allowing my pride to interfere with my encountering God. The Jesus tweaking Pastor Don somehow seemed much cooler now. I was at an event at school known as Identity Weekend. This was a deep training to learn who we are in Christ and who the world tries to make us. We purposefully reflected on our lives and our choices. We then repented for our sin. We broke off any evil soul ties or addictions. We especially forgave everybody who'd wronged us. Pastor showed us biblically that to hear God, we must tear down the wall of sin that separates us. To be blessed fully in the gifts of the Holy Spirit, we cannot live in unforgiveness. To walk in the giftings, we must be walking obediently with Christ. The class focused on these steps. Even though I thought I knew all of this from my heavenly hall pass experience, I still wasn't hearing God's voice, so I pressed into this teaching.

Pastor Don then proved biblically that our level of giftings is determined only by our level of faith. This caused me to laugh out loud. If that were true, I'd be walking on water. I had more faith than I knew. The pastor saw me getting frustrated, and he gently explained that I could know, but have no faith. This perplexed me. He said I could have great faith to know God was real, but I also needed faith to believe that He would work through me in miraculous ways to win hearts for Jesus. Wow, I'd never thought of it that way. I had shallow, kiddie pool, water wings, life jacket faith when it came to that. The pastor then explained the key to understanding this…God is not using me so I can be great, but so people can see how great God's love is. By healing the broken, God can use us to help build their faith. God wants to heal people; He loves drawing them to him through miraculous healing.

I was shown in heaven that every word in the Bible is true. I decided then and there that I was going to put aside my religious beliefs and start focusing on God's truth. By religious beliefs I mean, how we as the body of Christ, or the church often put God in a box because we don't expect miracles. We do expect grace, but not miracles. However, I was going to take off my water wings and climb out of the kiddie pool. I wanted to swim with sharks. As of that day, I decided to walk in complete faith. Folks already think I'm a crazy Jesus Freak, so I'm going to embrace it. The only thing I have to lose is my pride and arrogance. I've been trying to kill those things anyway. As I poured out my heart's desire to God in prayer amidst my classmates, I asked God, "Please Lord, is this why I haven't been able to finish my book? Is it because you want me to go deeper?" and for the first time since heaven, I clearly heard God say in my spirit, "Your book isn't finished because your story isn't over." I heard God and His voice was like healing rain in the desert of my thirsty heart.

Then He spoke again saying, "I brought you home to get your book off the shelf. Your story is to teach My people to use My power and walk in My anointing." It made perfect sense. So many people tell me they know my heaven story is true because the exact same thing happened to them. I felt there was no reason to even write this book because my story isn't unique anymore. I was only writing it because God had sent so many strangers to me telling me He wanted me to write a book. As I began to write about my new adventures in igniting the Holy Spirit's giftings, God started testing me in some crazy ways.

God doesn't test us because He wants to know our character. God tests us, so He can show us and others our character. Once I started exercising my hearing gift, it became strong quickly. God started giving me surprise assignments. In 2019, Tony and I were blessed to be at the KLOVE music fan awards show in Nashville, Tennessee. We were told God had a miracle there regarding my story. We cancelled a huge race weekend (a big sacrifice for Tony) and left for our greatest adventure yet.

Many miracles happened from the moment we arrived. I told

my husband I knew God was going to challenge me, and I could feel it coming. But the final morning at the Grand Ole Opryland Church service, I was relieved that the imminent testing was miscalculated. I'd made it through like a normal woman of God. During the worship of Lauren Daigle, praising God for the best weekend ever, God told me to go talk to the guy who just started preaching and tell him my story. I assured God when he was done preaching the sermon, if he came off the stage to greet the 5,000ish guests, I'd tell him my story. He was some big Christian Movie Producer (Alex Kendrick) who'd made some Christian hit movies. His movies are great but nothing like my story. Was God going to really make me bust through security to tell him my story? God said, "I told you to go tell him your story." I said, "Lord, surely you don't expect me to bust through security and climb onto the stage of the service?" God responded, "Do it now." So, I got up and told Tony, "God says I have to go tell that guy my story right now." My husband looked confused, he said, "What guy?" I said, "The guy preaching. I'll be right back." As I started searching for a backstage entrance and security personnel, I just took a deep breath and tried to focus. I passed three places that I expected big security to be posted, but nobody was there. I snuck up the backstage stairs like a ninja, took another deep breath and walked right up to one of the greatest singers of my time. I interrupted her saying, "Hi, excuse me Mrs. Daigle. I'm a big fan, and Mr. Kendrick, I'm sorry to interrupt you, but God told me to come and tell you something. Can we speak privately please?" His Holy Spirit filled eyes twinkled as he scanned the backstage for security. He guided me to a quiet place backstage. It was still insanely loud with worship, and I told him my story as quickly as possible. I then handed him my business card and thanked him for his kindness.

In less than six minutes I was back at my seat in the auditorium. Worship had just ended, and I found Tony who was nervously looking for me. Turns out we both expected me to be arrested or taken to the Opryland hoosegow. We got out of there as quickly as we could feeling like felons for Jesus. After doing

God's task, we were blessed with even more incredible miracles.

I had done many hard things after leaving Nashville, but the hardest by far was sharing my story at speaking gigs. The minute I shared getting to heaven and seeing the hole in Jesus' feet I'd start sobbing, get a huge lump in my throat, and start shaking. At the end of one of my meetings, a buddy sitting in the front pew started crying. It was my girlfriend's husband, who I thought was trying to nap. He is a big tough redneck, and he was sobbing. My friend explained that in the twenty years they'd been married, she'd never seen Richard cry.

He went outside and collected himself and came in sometime later. He sat back down and struggled to hold back his tears. He couldn't even speak and just held up his hands making a big circle with his thumbs and pointer fingers. Immediately I knew what was happening. He had been shown me clinging to the feet of Jesus and begging not to be sent away, screaming like a child being torn away from its mother at the Holocaust. When Richard could finally speak again, he described seeing things I'd never shared like how I hooked my right arm around Jesus' left ankle when I was being pulled away. He knew exactly how big the holes in Jesus' feet were, and everything I physically did to stay. He couldn't stop crying for me. He still can't speak about it, but the fact that someone understands how devastating that was for me is such a gift. The best part of that miracle, however, is that from that moment on, I can share my story without losing my voice, hyperventilating, or sobbing. I can smile and cherish all the wonders, without all the PTSD. God delivered me, I was not only healed that day, but God gave me a brother. Richard is fiercely protective of me now, and a big prayer support.

ACTIVATION

I watched several video teachings from Bethel Church on the gift of prophecy. Four people who never met me or each other from different times and places have told me essentially the same thing; that's not a coincidence. They stepped out in faith at the risk of being thought crazy to give me a message from God. None of them had been to heaven, but their faith was greater than mine. They acted in obedience; as a result, I was strengthened and blessed. I wanted desperately to do that for somebody, to hear God's voice and share His will for them, helping them walk in their giftings and callings. I knew God was speaking to others, so why not me? God thought I was worth bringing to heaven, and perhaps He had even more in store? The next class I felt ready to dive in.

After our video lesson, our teacher surprised us with what's called "activation." We were divided into groups of five and were told to put one person in the middle, and once this person's eyes were shut, the four others were to circle around until the person in the middle said, "Stop." While eyes were still closed, the person in the middle was to ask God prayerfully who was standing in front of them, and then ask for a word of knowledge for them from God. It felt like a spiritual game of Monkey in the Middle. How was I supposed to guess who was standing around me, and guess what God wanted me to say to these strangers? The teacher clarified that I was in no way to guess but to pray and see what

God said. Fortunately, I wasn't worried about looking silly. The teacher assured us God often speaks in whispers to our spirit. I volunteered to go first. I knew I'd probably blow this about four times, but I wanted to practice because hearing God's will was the whole point of this journey. My four classmates circled me and stopped. I cleared my head and listened to hear any whispers to my heart. I felt certain I knew who was standing before me. I thought it was Charlie; I felt sure this knowledge was from God because I couldn't think this stuff up. God showed me a man who looked in the mirror every day and felt as insignificant as a mouse in a maze, doing the same thing day after day and feeling small and unnecessary. But God saw him as a lion, brave and beautiful, a lion who carried God's light into the darkest places and scared demons.

I then turned, eyes still closed, and prayed again for God to give me a name and message. I felt that a woman was in front of me. In my mind, I saw her nametag, and I believed I was speaking to Cathy. God showed me she loved to garden and had been sowing seeds for some time, and it was finally harvest time. God showed me a sweet loving gardener whose flowers were His treasures. He said harvest time was now, and He was so grateful for her diligence and tender care of His garden. Her work was beautiful to Him; God knew the harvest was hard for her to tend, but He delighted in her harvest.

I then turned again, eyes closed tight, and "saw" Louise. I told her I saw suitcases packed and she was preparing for a trip. She was making demons fear her, a dragon slayer. Her journey was for God, and it would be fruitful.

Last, I turned and saw in my heart Carol. Carol was given gifts of language. She would be a translator for God. Interpretation of His Word would make people feel loved and at peace, welcomed, and wanted. It delighted God how she used this gift to show His love. I felt God's joy for her.

I told the group I was done. I was instructed by the staff to open my eyes. I was surprised to see my group grinning ridiculously at me. They explained that I got all four names and words of knowledge right. Charlie was looking at me stunned and speechless. The staff member asked them to interpret my words of knowledge starting with Carol. Carol explained that she worked with refugees helping them acclimate to our country. She loved sharing Jesus and the Bible with them. It was her passion. She was amazed that God had shown me that and that He was delighted in her efforts as she had just begun doing this and wasn't sure if it was a good fit and had been asking God if the people really were benefiting from her efforts. My word from God was confirmation that her efforts had God's attention.

Next Louise, whom I'd never heard speak in class, timidly explained that she was on a team of missionaries that would be traveling to a Third World country to raise people from the dead to build faith in a country that was deeply rooted in witchcraft. The only way to prove our God was real would be to do the impossible. God had shown me demons were aware she was coming, and they were frightened. Although I saw no bodies resurrected, I did see demons fleeing from her. I would have never guessed she could be a part of such a team. Knowing her efforts would be noticed in the spirit world and cause demons to fear, gave her great confidence.

Next was Cathy, the gardener. Cathy was probably in her early 60s. She explained that her ministry was visiting nursing homes. She'd been doing it for years. She would visit the elderly and share Jesus and His message with people who were lonely and rarely saw visitors. She would pour into them by bringing them flowers from her garden. She loved these people dearly but was greatly saddened that they all seemed to be dying. I was able to encourage her through my message from God that they were His beautiful harvest. Her pouring into their lives was like she was tending God's flower garden, and her flowers were now adorning heaven.

Next was Charlie who was absolutely shocked by my message. Charlie explained that he was just a custodian at the state mental hospital. God saw Charlie as a lion, carrying His light into the darkest places. Charlie explained that His wife had told him that morning that he may think he's just a mouse, but God knows he's a lion. Her words that only he knew were affirmed by God. He may feel his life is small and unnoticed, but his love and kindness in sharing Jesus to the patients at the state mental hospital was driving out the darkness of evil. He was a mighty humble man in God's eyes. God loved and respected his humble heart.

The following week in class was a surprise field trip. My ADHD was thrilled to go on an adventure. My newfound acceptance of Holy Spirit giftings was glowing in me until I heard our task. We were told to break up into groups of three, including one staff member and two students. We were to pray separately and ask God for three strangers to pray with three descriptions of them, where to find them, and what they needed prayer for. We were given a slip of paper to write down any information God gave us.

Before I got deep into praying, God gave me the first name, David, and I asked God for a description. God showed me denim shorts and a dark jacket, dark salt and pepper facial hair, and a blue ball cap on his head. I assumed this was my imagination but asked for more. I then felt my thighs burning. I wrote down the description and asked for another person to pray for. God told me Evan. He showed me a skinny, bundled up little man, probably 60ish. He looked homeless and God showed me he was a slave to alcohol, and felt broken and abandoned by everybody and betrayed his family. The last person God gave me was Ethan, I thought. He was a huge guy with gray basketball shorts and youngish. God showed me he was angry, and it caused him migraines. The download took less than three minutes. He even told me two locations nearby where I would find these guys.

My team came to me, sad they had not been given a download, but I sheepishly explained I had three, but it was probably my wishful imagination. I showed them my sheet and said we needed to go to Walgreens first, so we hopped in a car and left for the store. I was a nervous wreck. My legs were starting to burn, so I knew we were looking for David, the man in the denim shorts. I had my clipboard in hand and started scanning the store with the team. I circled the store and prayed for about fifteen minutes and grew discouraged. The team met, and we discussed looping the store again and praying we'd meet David before moving on to the Dollar Tree. A teammate bumped me excitedly as we rounded the isle; there at the far end of the store stood exactly as I had described him to my team. I shouted, "David." The man looked at me as I ran towards him like a charging bull. He said, "Do I know you?" I said, "Is your name David?" He said, "Yes, do I know you?" I explained that God told me to come to Walgreens and pray for his thighs. He quickly backed away from me, and he was not in the least bit interested in me putting my hands on his thighs and praying. I briefly explained my mission, but he refused. I pleaded for him to let me pray over him. My legs felt as if they were on fire, but poor David thought he was being pranked on a hidden camera show.

I kindly left David blankly staring at the cough drops. I said I'd hang around for a bit in case he changed his mind. I wandered the store for about ten minutes, checking in occasionally with David who hadn't moved from that spot. I wasn't going to get to lay hands on David or his thighs. I felt God nudging me to move on, so I returned to David, still staring blankly at the cough drops. I explained that I was sorry I scared him, but God was pursuing him. I explained I was praying he would know how loved he was by God for Him to send me to find him. I also explained before leaving that I didn't have to put my hands on him for God to heal him. I then left him dazed and confused in Walgreens.

I couldn't wait to get to the Dollar Tree to pray over the next two people. On the drive to Dollar Tree, my partners tried to get me to approach the next person with a bit less fervor, and I prayed for God's help to calm down. We arrived and walked the small store for about ten minutes. We regrouped fruitless, so my partners again looked at my paper I'd filled out. I'd written that Evan was homeless, so we decided to stand in front of the store and look. I said his name may not have been Evan and showed them how both Evan and Ethan had a question mark next to their names. As I was praying, Evan came into sight, walking towards me. He was exactly as God showed me...tiny, old, and bundled with layers of clothing. My chest started burning with love and compassion for this man. I approached him gently and asked if his name was Evan, and he said no, but I remained certain he was the man I was to pray for. He said, "I'm Kevin." Close enough. I shared with him how passionately God loves him. It was clear Kevin felt abandoned by all love. He cried as I proved God was pursuing him by Him sending us there. I hugged Kevin as my team and I prayed over him. We helped Kevin accept Christ and then prayed to break off all chains of bondage and addiction. It was beautiful seeing Kevin feel God's tremendous affection for him and realize God was fighting for his soul. As my team listened to Kevin's story, I noticed the other man that God clearly showed me getting out of his car. As he approached the store, my head started to hurt. I knew this had to be Ethan. I hugged Kevin and said I'd continue to pray for him.

While the team stayed with Kevin, Ethan walked up to the front of the store, and I asked "Hi, are you Ethan?" He responded, "No, mam." I was confused as this was the guy God showed me clear down to his gray basketball shorts and socks with sandals. So, I asked him, "What's your name?" He was in an obvious hurry and found my curiosity an inconvenience. He replied, "Ian." Close enough. I quickly explained that I knew he had terrible headaches and God wanted to heal him. God sent me to pray over him to build his faith. He needed to know God was pursuing him and loved him deeply. Ian explained he had to get home immediately to his sick baby. He was only there for medicine. I smiled and said, "No worries, I would be praying for him."

Such a phenomenal evening that an hour prior I was dreading. I had to trust the things I was seeing were from God and not my imagination. In two hours, I had heard God, stepped out in faith, and told three strangers God wanted to heal them because He loved them deeply. I know when these three men are meeting Jesus in heaven, I will be a part of their story.

That evening when I was putting on my pajamas, my thighs were still on fire. I looked at them, and they were red and splotchy like they were infected. I took a picture to show my friends. Not only could I feel David's pain, I could physically see it. I knew God was reminding me to continue to pray. I got on my knees and prayed over David until my thighs felt normal again.

CURTAIN CALL

Why hadn't I ever studied in church or Sunday school that Jesus left us with a gift so powerful that we could perform miracles to win souls for Him? Jesus says we can do greater things than Him, but I always believed those miracles were only offered over 2,000 years ago. I had been to heaven and had walked through every day of Jesus' life before His crucifixion, so I had no excuse for believing that lie. When Jesus taught us to pray, He said, "Thy Kingdom come, thy will be done, on earth as it is in heaven." The key to walking in God's presence, so we can do God's will on earth as it is in heaven is to align our character with Jesus'. For me it means constantly consuming God's truth by reading my Bible daily, so I'm reminding myself of how Jesus would respond. It means choosing to show love even when I disagree. Sometimes that looks like thanking God for failed relationships, losses and loneliness, as well as our unanswered prayers. Fully surrendering to God means we know all things work together for His good. I now co-labor with friends who will lovingly call me into accountability when my character doesn't represent the character of Christ.

I'm not proud that it took me 20 years after heaven to realize that I was stifling the Holy Spirit. I thought that immeasurable love was the only really tangible gift the Holy Spirit had for me. I thought I knew God's truths because I was in a culture of believers who memorized God's words but didn't pursue God's promises. Even worse, I judged. I was a Pharisees even after heaven. Once I realized I had been believing lies, I experienced freedom at levels I formerly thought only existed in heaven.

I was frustrated with God for so many years. Even though I had faith and love, I didn't like how He went about sending me back. But looking back now, it's obvious that nothing Jesus could have said or done would have made me comfortable with leaving Him. So now I'm praising God for sending me back.

Please indulge me for a few minutes. I'd like to have you close your eyes, quiet your heart, and imagine at this very moment you're arriving in heaven. You're overwhelmed with joy and peace, and your brain and body are fully alive and functioning. You've never imagined feeling this good and loved. You realize all of what you're experiencing for the first time is happening because of where you are. You are in heaven and kneeling at the feet of the one who died just so you could be there. He shows you your entire life, nothing hidden or deleted. Then as you're processing how trivial your trials on Earth were and how you allowed them to distract you from everything that truly matters, Jesus again shows you your entire lifetime but through the eyes of your Creator. You see how skillfully and tenderly He made you. He delights even in your flaws; you are His masterpiece. Every day of your life you see that Jesus was beside you, loving you, holding you, telling you that you're not alone. You see your Garment of Glory start to twinkle and sparkle as you get older. You begin to realize how much your Jesus protected you and how endless His love is for you. You wonder how you never felt Him beside you when you so desperately wanted to, and you see that it was you that created the barriers that made Him harder to hear and feel. As you're trying to process how He could love you so deeply, Jesus takes you through His entire life. You watch all of heaven grieve His leaving, and you see God's heart breaking because of what Jesus chose to do for you. God loves you enough to let Jesus do it. You see Jesus' entire life of passionately pursuing His Father's will. You see Jesus in the dessert, hot, thirsty, and starving. You see Him resist unimaginable temptations, and you watch His best friends betray Him. He washed their feet and loved them anyway. You want so badly to stop the soldiers beating your Jesus, and you feel the spatter of His blood from the whip splash across your face. You don't want to watch or hear this, but Jesus is staring at you with so much love, you can't turn away. With all His strength, He opens His eyes, and trembling He lifts His head. He stares into your eyes and tries to force a smile to end your suffering and whispers, "I choose You." You sob uncontrollably because He has done nothing to deserve this, and He has the power to stop it but refuses because He loves you. You watch His slow painful death helplessly.

Then you're back in heaven at Jesus' perfectly pierced feet, feeling a level of happiness, safety, and belonging, that you never knew existed. You are full known, and completely loved, when Jesus says you can't stay – you only had a hall pass and now need to go back and share His goodness.

* * *

I'd like to pray for you now, and I'd like to give you a piece of heaven:

Father God, I humbly ask you to create in me and my reader a pure heart oh God and renew a steadfast spirit within us. Lord I pray that my reader will choose to seek your truth and your intimacy in a quiet place. I ask you to give us hearts that passionately pursue you above all else. I ask You to fill us with your powerful Holy Spirit, so we can walk in our full anointing you created us to have. I ask you to help us lean into You, to hear Your whispers, rather than the evil one's shouts. I ask You to pour more of your gifts of the Spirit into us and use us to increase the occupancy of Your Kingdom in significant ways. I ask You to give us the wisdom and gratitude and tenacity to steward what You've already given us, so we can receive more. I pray that You will bless us with friends who love and seek You above all else. I ask You to fill us with gratitude for Your sacrifice, regardless of

123

our situation. I ask you to protect us from the plots and lies of the enemy, so we will not be easily knocked down. I ask You to fill us with Your love for Your people. I pray You will bless us and their future generations to be constantly in Your holy presence. In Jesus' mighty name, Amen.

This life's going to be tough, and there's sure to be storms, but if we put our faith in the One who died for us, we'll never be alone. If we let Jesus be our best friend, He can calm the storm or teach us to walk on water.

Please come find me in heaven and give me a hug. I'll be the one sitting on an upside-down bucket holding a cardboard sign that says, "Welcome Home."

Made in United States
Troutdale, OR
07/01/2023

10908468R00076